I TRUST TO BE BELIEVED

I TRUST TO BE BELIEVED

BY

ELMER L. ANDERSEN

former Governor
of Minnesota

edited by

Lori Sturdevant

NODIN PRESS

ISBN 1-932472-07-X

Nodin Press is a division of Micawbers, Inc.
530 N Third Street
Suite 120
Minneapolis, MN 55401

DEDICATION

To the people of Minnesota, who have given me opportunities for growth, development and service for more than 75 years.

"In coming among you to assume the position I hold, I trust to be believed when I say that I brought with me only the sincere determination to do right, to do justice, to live in harmony with all, and to use whatever power I incidentally possess, entirely for the true and abiding weal of Minnesota."

—Gov. Alexander Ramsey,
concluding remarks,
first gubernatorial address to the Minnesota territorial
House of Representatives,
September 3, 1849

CONTENTS

IV. EDUCATION

V. WORLD CITIZENSHIP

VI. FUNDAMENTALS

Author's Preamble

One day in 2002, Annie Klessig, a person we had retained to bring some order out of the big accumulation of papers and reports and books and things that were remaining in our home office, came upon a folder of manuscript speeches. She read one of them and was impressed with it, and called it to the attention of my personal assistant, Ani Sorenson. "I wonder if Elmer has seen any of these lately?" she asked.

Of course, I hadn't. I hardly knew they existed. Ani read a few of them, and was particularly taken with one I gave to a women's organization, the Altrusa Club, in 1950. It included themes that foreshadowed the women's movement that blossomed twenty years later. Ani said, "You've got to talk to Lori about these." So we communicated with Lori Sturdevant, who did such a wonderful job as editor of *A Man's Reach*. She too became enthusiastic about the manuscripts. And that was how this book was born.

I had spoken to audiences extemporaneously for so long, in part because of the loss of my eyesight due to macular degeneration, that I had forgotten that there was a time when I used manuscripts. We have come upon about fifty of them, mostly from the 1950s and 1960s. We also located video and audio tapes of more recent speeches and public comments. As we reviewed them, we found many that contained comments about issues that are still challenging to Minnesotans. We were struck by the consistency of those comments through the years. In many cases, calls that were made forty and fifty years ago for a particular policy or course of action are still relevant today.

We have a wonderful state, and we want to keep it that way. Our sense of direction may have faltered of late. Showing today's Minnesotans the roots of an idea that was judged worthy forty or fifty years ago, and that still pertains to our shared experience, may be useful. That is my hope for this collection.

I owe thanks to my wife Eleanor. In this project, and in everything else in my life, for more than seventy years, she has played the preeminent role. I also have appreciated the other friends and family who have read portions of the book and given helpful comments. Particularly, I owe much to the skill of Lori Sturdevant as editor, who finds a way to meld what I say today with what I said years ago into a coherent whole. I can't say enough about Lori's skill as a friend and collaborator, more than simply as an editor.

Former U. S. Senator Eugene McCarthy does me great honor with his kind words in this book's introduction. For his contribution and friendship through more than fifty years, I am most grateful.

—Elmer L. Andersen
August 2003

Editor's Foreword

One can only imagine the poignancy of the moment in September 1849 when the new territory of Minnesota inaugurated its first governor. Alexander Ramsey took the oath of office, then did what comes naturally to politicians at special moments great and small: He gave a speech. He must have been keenly conscious of the history he was making. He must have wanted to communicate his understanding of the gravity of his task, and convey an assurance that he possessed the virtues, values and ability to see it through. But he dared not lapse into pomposity or pretense. He likely was a familiar figure to everyone within earshot. He was surrounded by people with whom he had close relationships of mutual reliance. He was obliged to speak nobly but humbly, friend to friend. He said, "I trust to be believed."

Elmer L. Andersen has long admired Ramsey's choice of those words that day, so much so that he recited them in his own inaugural address 112 years later. For more than 50 years, Andersen has been speaking to Minnesota audiences, friend to friend. There may be no other living Minnesotan who has known his fellow citizens better, or is better known by them, than the former governor affectionately known as "Elmer L."

I Trust to Be Believed is the by-product of the unique relationship that ties Minnesota's thirtieth governor with the state that he chose as his own seventy-five years ago. Since he first ran for the state Senate in 1949, Elmer has loved meeting and speaking to Minnesotans, and they in turn have enjoyed hearing his warmth and wisdom. Through all his many careers —in government, business, education, agriculture, journalism, philanthropy and more—he has been in demand as a public speaker. He made speeches several times a day as a candidate, almost daily while a state senator and governor, and at least weekly as he led campaigns for enactment of the taconite amendment, creation of Voyageurs National Park, and an endowment for the University of Minnesota. The give-and-take between speaker and audience became part of the rhythm of Andersen's life. Thankfully, the beat goes on in his ninety-fifth year.

No written or recorded trace exists of many of the speeches Andersen delivered to Minnesotans. Early in his political career he ceased relying on written manuscripts when he addressed audiences. He preferred to speak from memory, without notes, so that he could gaze steadily into the faces of his listeners and pick up on their reactions to his words. During his governorship, and in the years since, only a few special speeches were recorded and later transcribed. That's why Elmer was surprised when his staff reported that they had found a quantity of notes and manuscripts sufficient to be compiled into a book. But he soon acknowledged that with the addition of some manuscripts on file at the library of the Minnesota Historical Society, and a number of more recent addresses preserved on audio and video tape, the question was not "Is there enough?" but "What to choose?"

Our choices were guided by a desire to produce a volume not of history or reminiscence, but of contemporary relevance. Elmer views life's purpose as service. He aims to provide something useful to his fellow citizens. We sought to produce a collection of commentary on current topics, drawing on ideas and insights that have stood the test of time. For that reason, the speeches we selected are organized by theme rather than by date. Our goal is not to preserve a record of Andersen the speaker, but to present anew Andersen the inspiration.

Though the speeches in this collection span fifty-four years, from 1949 to 2003, there is a consistency about them that I find both remarkable and reassuring. The young man of vision is now the old man of experience. The strong voice that struck a chord with Minnesotans in the 1950s now creaks with age. But it is still the same voice, articulating the same values and principles. Elmer L. Andersen is the touchstone of the Minnesota spirit. He is still calling his listeners to be the best they can be, and to join forces in building the best state Minnesota can be. His call is still compelling.

The comments that follow were taken from conversations Elmer and I had in 2002 and 2003. The speeches have been drawn from both manuscripts and transcriptions of recorded addresses. Throughout this volume, the speeches are printed in one type-face, while the comments that precede them are in another. An arrow indicates the point where a speech begins.Some of them have been shortened but none have been significantly altered in other ways. The language was not edited to reflect changes in cultural mores or attitudes. We chose to keep it true to its period, though we wince with our readers at language that to twenty-first century ears sounds excessively oriented toward males, or toward America's white majority. Whenever possible, the date on which a speech was first presented is cited. In a few cases, only the month or the year of a speech is known.

This project drew support from many quarters. I echo Elmer's thanks to his wife Eleanor. She has graciously opened her home to me and my family, and helped us as reader, counselor and friend. Likewise, Elmer's staff provided assistance in numerous ways, from finding material to serving cookies and coffee during Saturday work sessions. Ani Sorenson, Elmer's chief personal assistant, was an originator of this project and its great booster and helpmate. We owe much to her.

Most of the materials for this book, including all of the photographs, were drawn from Elmer's personal collection. Some speeches from his governorship, 1961-63, were found at the Minnesota Historical Society library. We retrieved a smattering of additional information with the help of the Minneapolis Star Tribune newspaper library and the Evangelical Lutheran Church in America archives. Outstanding assistance in transcribing audio tapes came from our good friend Beverly Hermes, who was also a crucial partner in producing Elmer's autobiography, *A Man's Reach*. Tim O'Brien and Marlene James of the *Star Tribune* editorial staff were very helpful in transforming yellowing manuscript pages into modern Microsoft Word files.

It is a pleasure to work on this project with Norton Stillman, publisher of Nodin Press, and his editor John Toren. We are grateful for their enthusiastic embrace of our project. Nodin Press also produced a collection of Elmer's editorials, *Views from the Publisher's Desk*, in 1997.

My partner Martin Vos; my children, Ted, John and Emelia Carroll; their father, Hobson Carroll, and my colleagues at the Star Tribune have all provided sustaining support in this effort. But my largest debt is owed to Elmer Andersen. For the privilege of helping him continue more than a half-century of useful communication with Minnesotans, and for the honor of his friendship, I will be forever grateful.

—Lori Sturdevant
September 2003

Introduction

by former U. S. Senator Eugene McCarthy

I Trust to Be Believed," a phrase from the address given to the territorial government of Minnesota on the third of September in 1849 by Governor Alexander Ramsey, is a fitting title for a collection of speeches and commentaries by Governor Elmer L. Andersen. Much as Ramsey did on that day, Elmer directs his messages primarily at citizens, rather than office-holders. But he would say, citing his own record, that among the duties of citizens are the seeking and holding of public office, and participation in partisan politics and political activities.

It was in the fields of partisan politics that Governor Andersen and I first met. He is a Republican; I, a Democrat. We never ran against each other for the same office, but he helped manage the campaign of my opponent in 1948; part of his state Senate district overlapped my congressional district; and he ran for governor in 1960 when I was a first-term U. S. senator. We shared platforms, but more often kitchen duties, at county fairs, festivals, and various "days"—Corn Days, Sauerkraut Days, and the like. Most memorable to me were the county fairgrounds in southern Minnesota when, at odd hours, there were no people on the grounds except Elmer, me, and a few men or boys spraying animals to keep them cool.

I hear the cadences of the speeches we gave at those events in the pages of this volume. Various phrases and words mark these speeches as those of one Minnesotan addressing another. For example, some things are "not worth a hill of beans." We must "gather our wits" and "get going." We are "pinched for funds," and we must be prepared for "the long haul." The governor will "visit the people" and be "visited" by them.

His messages go far beyond the homespun, however. These speeches reflect Governor Andersen's sensitivity to the constitutional separation of powers under the federal government, and to the distinction between the federal and state governments. He demonstrates an intuitive understanding and support for the argument made by Alexander Hamilton in Federalist Papers Number Seventeen, in response to the charge that under the proposed constitution, the federal government might become so powerful that it would absorb "those residual authorities" better left with the states. "Allowing the utmost latitude to the love of power which any reasonable man can require," Hamilton wrote, "I am at a loss to discover what temptation the persons entrusted with the administration of the general government could ever feel to divest the states of authorities of that description."

Hamilton—and Andersen—may not have foreseen the competition that has arisen today between the states and the federal government over matters of education, health care, crime control and more. Presidential candidates now declare that they will be known as "the education president," while governors in increasing numbers present themselves as presidential candidates. The blurring of jurisdictional roles has led to irresponsible and no-fault government. Andersen's message about the rightful separation of powers is appropriate today.

Included in this volume are speeches about civil rights that Andersen made more than forty years ago, at a time when racial justice had not been advanced by federal legislation. At issue in 1959 was the building of Interstate 94 through the city of St. Paul, and the accompanying problems of the destruction of a largely segregated African-American neighborhood, and the relocation of its residents. Governor Andersen's presentation before the City Council of St. Paul that May was a powerful force in reconciling the different views. He made the compelling argument: "If we are willing to force a man to sell his home to build a highway, we should not balk at prohibiting voluntary sales in a manner hurtful to society." Ultimately, neighborhood interests were protected, while the threat of continuing segregation was overcome.

Elmer's participation in this case was characteristic. He often sought to accomplish at least two aims simultaneously: the immediate one, building the highway, and the supplemental, longer-term one, eliminating or preventing segregation. This collection of speeches includes other examples of his application of this rule of action. At a speech at a Lutheran seminary, for example, he addressed the bearing of religion both on private life and on society. He made particular mention of toleration, with emphasis on the need and responsibility for Christians to understand the religion and culture of Muslims.

He includes a speech he gave in the early 1950s to the Minnesota Boy Scouts, generally commending them, but he adds in his "afterthoughts" his disapproval of the Scouts' more recent action barring gays from their ranks.

And he includes a most contemporary commentary on the war in Iraq. Elmer is rightfully critical of the restraint on civil liberties and rights in the name of national security since September 11, 2001. In this regard, he is in good company, restating a warning sounded by Alexis de Tocqueville 180 years ago.

More than a farewell address, this book is a most worthy achievement, of both historical value and relevance to current problems. I trust to be believed when I recommend it to readers.

—Eugene J. McCarthy
October 1, 2003

I TRUST TO BE BELIEVED

POLITICS AND GOVERNING

INAUGURAL ADDRESS

The privilege of delivering an inaugural address as governor has been granted so far to only thirty-eight men in Minnesota history. One would think that opportunity would stand in my memory as a high moment. But the truth is that my inaugural message to the legislature was one of many high moments in a rush of activity at the start of 1961. Events hurled themselves at me, and I had to respond without the care that one would like. I remember that time mostly as an exhilarating, exhausting blur.

The highlight of my inaugural period may have been the Tournament of Roses parade and the Rose Bowl game in Pasadena, California, on January 2. (New Year's Day fell on a Sunday that year.) I was officially representing Minnesota because the University of Minnesota Golden Gopher football team had won the Big Ten title, and was playing in the Rose Bowl. Minnesota lost that game to the University of Washington, but the Gophers made a return trip to the Rose Bowl in 1962, and defeated UCLA that year. A Minnesota team hasn't been back to the Rose Bowl since. I always say that it only goes to show what a good governor can do for the University!

Only two days later, I was standing in front of a joint session of the legislature, discussing all manner of weighty state policy issues. In those years of two-year terms, in inaugural years, governors did not give State of the State speeches to describe policy initiatives. Inaugural speeches were long, policy-laden addresses, frequently taking more than an hour to deliver. Ordinarily, I wrote my own speeches, but in this instance, I was more the chief editor than the chief author. My team of policy advisers wrote various sections, and I rephrased them to fit my speaking style.

Much of what I said was particular to contemporary issues that have since faded in importance. But some themes endure. One is my belief that Minnesota is best governed when the tripartite division of authority envisioned in our constitution is respected. The legislature makes the laws, the judiciary interprets them, and the executive carries them out. Legislators have become very deferential to governors as policy-setters. That is an abdication of their rightful role. It is true that people look to the governor for leadership. I was faulted as governor, and perhaps deservedly so, for bending over too far in respecting the role of the legislature. But if I erred in giving the legislature too much rein, I would submit that today in St. Paul, there is a tendency to err in the opposite direction. It is the legislature's function to establish a state position on public matters, not to rubber-stamp a position staked out by the governor.

My inaugural message had a long section on economic development. I share some of it here because securing prosperity for Minnesota remains a leading obligation of state government. I spoke then about an economy that was very reliant on Minnesota's natural resources—agriculture, minerals, timber. While those resources remain important to the state's economic base, their dominance has diminished in the ensuing forty years, as the manufacturing and service sectors have grown. Today a speech such as this one would certainly mention the need to focus on high-technology industries, and would call for support for our colleges and universities to provide both training and research for the economy's technology sector. Investment of that sort is crucial to the state's economic health—more so than is recognized by the business lobbyists who are forever calling for lower taxes.

Here is a portion of my inaugural address:

⏭ I am deeply honored to become the thirtieth governor of the state of Minnesota. I have taken the oath of office with deep respect for the responsibilities involved. May I congratulate you, as members of the sixty-second Legislature, on your important role in government for the next two years.

I have great respect for the legislative branch of government. I have an equal respect for the judicial and executive branches of government. I will respect the prerogatives of each. You [legislators] have the responsibility of formulating the policies of the government, of making the appropriations for state services and of levying the taxes to carry on the programs provided. As chief executive I have some share in the formulation of those policies, and the task of directing the administrative functions to implement the policies decided upon.

May I say that my approach will not be one of extreme partisanship. It never has been. It will be my purpose to work with both groups of both houses, and with every individual legislator in achieving constructive legislation.

I am convinced that our people want and are willing to support a strong elementary and secondary school system; they are proud of our great university; they realize the importance of the state colleges and junior colleges. Likewise we want an excellent mental health program, a forward-looking correctional program, fine highways, humanitarian welfare programs, and all the other essential services state and local government provide. However, it is essential that we have jobs and payrolls if we are to have the revenue to support all this.

We must give particular attention in this session to matters affecting the business and economic development of our state. Plentiful jobs at good pay are essential to the happiness and well-being of our people, and certainly essential to the fiscal soundness of any governmental program. It will be the purpose of this administration to give particular attention to the agricultural economy of our state, to emphasize greater research, marketing and promotion efforts, and accelerated business development, to provide new outlets for crops, livestock, and poultry.

Minnesota's greatest resource is the quality, skill, and ingenuity of its people. Under the operation of the Selective Service Act, Minnesota had the lowest rejection rate in the entire country. As our young people reported for the draft, they were healthier, better educated, and better adjusted than the young people of any other state. This is but one evidence of the superiority we can claim for our people. It is not surprising then that firms that started in Minnesota many years ago have risen to preeminence in their field.

In recent years some of these firms have felt it necessary to expand their operations in states other than Minnesota, and we have lost many job opportunities as a result. In one five-year period, four large Minnesota firms increased employment in Minnesota by 3,000 jobs while increasing employment outside of Minnesota by over 13,000 jobs. If we cannot retain the growth and expansion of firms already here, how can we expect to bring in new?

Industry has become mobile. It goes where it is wanted. It goes where it can operate to competitive advantage. We must recognize that industrial competition is more severe today than ever in history. Time was when U. S. concerns competed with foreign concerns for foreign markets. Today our concerns are competing with foreign manufacturers for our own market. Look about you and observe the products of foreign manufacture at every hand. We want to see the rest of the world develop economically and industrially. It is the best hope of future peace. If we are to share in this international development our firms must compete effectively, and therefore they seek locations where tax climates, availability of workers and natural resources, closeness to markets, all provide the advantages they need. Here again, this legislature could render a very great service to the people of our state by recognizing the realities, expressing concern, and taking steps to make Minnesota more attractive to manufacturing industry.

If we can aid our farmers in marketing the production of their efforts at better prices, if we can revitalize the mining industry, if we can come closer to realizing the potential of our forestry area, if we can more effectively bring thousands of tourists to our state to enjoy the beauty of our natural resources, if we can encourage more industry to expand and come to Minnesota, if our retailers, wholesalers and all other segments of our economy do well, we will have a flow of wealth into and around Minnesota that will make possible the standards of public service we all want to have and enjoy.

It would take a good deal longer to outline our many strengths, our great advantages, the fine opportunities that are ours, the blessings we all enjoy. Against that background, we should not be the least bit discouraged about the problems that look to us for solution. We should not be surprised if there are differences of opinion as to how we should go about the job ahead of us. The art of legislation is not in avoiding differences but in reconciling them. In any way at all that I can be of assistance to any one of you, personally or in any other way, I am at your service.

I could mean no concluding words more sincerely than those Alexander Ramsey used when he concluded the first inaugural address before the first Territorial Assembly on September 4, 1849. Here is what he said:

"In coming among you to assume the position I hold, I trust to be believed when I say, that I brought with me only the sincere determination to do right, to do justice, to live in harmony with all, and to use whatever power I incidentally possess, entirely for the true and abiding weal of Minnesota. And may that God who rules the destiny of nations, so prosper your doings and mine...that we will all bear with us the conviction that each performed his whole duty...for the people's true happiness, and the enduring glory of the American name."

—12:30 p.m., January 4, 1961

PRECINCT CAUCUSES—WHERE IT ALL BEGINS

Minnesota's system of organizing political parties with precinct caucuses has weakened in recent years. In 2002, only a few thousand people attended those neighborhood meetings that start the political parties' process of selecting candidates and writing a platform.

It's a change I regret. I think that precinct caucuses, and the party endorsement process they initiate, provide a wonderful method of choosing candidates for office. It's a process that allows for candidates to be screened time and time again by succeeding groups of party participants before the primary election. It also produces a platform that reflects the local situation, and provides a basis for holding elected officials accountable to their constituents.

One reason the caucuses declined in popularity with the broad population is that they became the tool of people with special interests. A well-organized group can take over caucuses and push aside those who are not part of their group. That happened in many places around the issue of abortion. Those who wanted to serve the people broadly no longer felt welcome, and stopped attending. The result has been a trend toward one-issue parties, which is no way to serve a big democracy.

Though many people now want to scrap the precinct caucus system, there is still a chance to reawaken it, and make it work once more. All a renewal would require is an influx of people who want to do something about government, not just complain about it. An active person who is willing to do some organizing can take over almost any precinct. A group of such individuals can put the people, not the politicians, in charge, and make the party an organization of the people rather than the professional promoters of a candidate.

American citizenship requires more than sitting back and choosing between programs and policies drawn up by a few. Citizens should also be involved in developing a people's program, from the grassroots. We've come to think of the government as *they*, as some onerous tax-absorbing unit, unfriendly and difficult to work with. We tend to elect people, then sit back and wait for them to do everything. It would make an enormous difference in our country if people understood that every person is a part of the government. The United States was founded on the assumption that people are equipped and able to produce and to run themselves a government that will serve them well. Fulfilling that responsibility should be part of the American way of life.

Minnesota's precinct caucus system has always needed promotion to work well, even when caucuses drew people by the tens of thousands rather than the handful. That was my mission when I spoke to a Washington County Republican rally in March 1950. Here is some of what I said:

⏭ The most important Republican date in 1950 in Minnesota is not the final election day of November 7, nor the primary date of September 12, but the precinct caucus day of March 13. If the challenge of March 13 is met, results on the following dates are bound to be favorable. If there is failure on March 13 then the job for success in the later dates is increased many fold.

Very few people know what a precinct caucus is. It is the Minnesota counterpart of the town meeting of New England. It is at the precinct caucus that the foundation of the party organization rests, that the authority of the party is determined and that principles to be written into platform find their geneses.

The precinct caucus determines whether a party shall be truly representative, or whether it will be controlled by a limited few. Likewise it determines whether participation in a party's activities is going to be general, or limited to a very few.

The people who come to your precinct caucus are your best source for block and township workers later on. If people come in at the very beginning and feel that they have a share in the setting up of the party mechanism and the determining of party policy, they are then willing to go out and work for that policy. It is much less easy to approach them in the fall to put the party program or the party slate across if they have had little part in developing it. It is a certainty that if you have a good crowd out at a precinct caucus, a good discussion of issues, send a strong slate to your county convention and set up a strong precinct committee, you are well on the way toward victory in the fall.

Even though all of you have probably had experience at precinct caucuses, it may not be amiss to review a little of the mechanics. Usually the caucus is held at the regular polling place in the precinct. The meeting is usually opened by the precinct chairman elected two years before. The first item of business is the election of a caucus chairman. The next order of business is selection of the delegates and alternates to the county convention, the number from your precinct being determined by your vote in the gubernatorial election of two years previous. Often, the previous precinct committee will have met prior to the caucus to draw up a slate of people who have shown their interest by working and who have indicated they can attend the county convention if elected. That slate will be placed in nomination. From that point, it is open for nominations from the floor. Campaigning at a caucus is without restriction. The voting is by ballot, and the preparation of ballots for a particular slate ahead of time is permitted. Blank ballots are supplied if contesting factions do not make up their own ballots ahead of time.

After the election of the delegates and alternates, a precinct committee of not less than five should be voted upon and the chairman indicated. The setting up of the precinct committee is often omitted and it is one of the most important parts of the caucus because with that precinct committee rests the responsibility of Republican activity in that two years. It is the one way and the only way to focus responsibility for party activity in the precinct. At some stage in the proceedings, the precinct chairman elected two years earlier should be called upon for a report of his committee's activities. It is like a report to the stockholders on the stewardship of the party during the two-year period.

If, from this outline, you see the possibilities that attend an effective precinct caucus, and would like to make it work in your precinct, all you have to do is go to work. You might call a meeting of your neighbors and tell them about the precinct caucus, line up several who would like to go, and in that way build your own slate of people to go to the county convention. You might line yourself up, if you will, as precinct chairman to be chosen at the caucus. One person with no great effort can assume and achieve leadership of his party in his precinct. It's one of the most satisfying political jobs a person can ever have and truly the most important job.

Once when Theodore Roosevelt was entering on a campaign for the presidency, a friend of his, of importance, asked him what he could do to aid in his election. He calmly waited for the answer, probably expecting to be invited to take some high-sounding title in the overall campaign organization. After a moment's hesitation, President Roosevelt turned to him and asked, "Can you carry your own precinct?" After all, the secret of any election victory is simply carrying your own precinct.

Now, the all-important question: How do you convince people to go to their caucus? I recommend going quietly to your neighbors and discussing issues with them individually. For example, in talking to a housewife or a worker, you could point out that a commission of able people recently made a study of spending by the executive branch of the federal government and found countless ways to save money without restricting services, simply by making sensible economies. You might say, everything the government purchases is through a purchase order. So complicated has the procedure become that it costs $10 to issue a purchase order. Yet, one-half of all the purchase orders are for material costing less than $10. One half of all the purchase orders cost more to issue than the material to be bought. Mr. Householder, it just doesn't make sense that your tax dollars should support that kind of inefficient program. There is only one reply that the person can make, and that is to say that of course it does not make sense, but what can we do about it? Well, Mr. Householder, we can start right in our own precinct at a caucus, discussing this and other matters that simply don't make sense.

The next person you talk to might well be an individual who says, "Well, I'm an independent voter." That's something to clear up: Who are Republicans and who are not? The fact is that a person's party affiliation is determined at the primary election. A person becomes a member of the party whose ballot he votes at the primary election. That's the only test of whether a person can attend a Republican caucus or not. Did he vote Republican at the last primary election? Then he is a Republican, and should attend our caucus and help formulate the policies and program of our party.

If you believe in free enterprise, if you believe in the importance of an individual in a democracy, if you believe everything is not as it should be, the one and only place for you to do something about it is at your precinct caucus. It's the most important political job in the whole works.

—March 2, 1950

THE IMPORTANCE OF THE PARTY SYSTEM

One of the biggest changes in American politics in the past forty years has been the diminution of the role and responsibility of political parties. Candidates today often run with little connection to their parties. They are free agents, accountable more to the special interests that finance their campaigns than to the political party they profess to represent. They make up their own campaign strategies using experts from other parts of the country—tricks of the trade that aim to fool and mislead the voters rather than inform them. TV commercials have replaced conversations with citizens. I don't think democracy is better as a result.

Campaigns in the 1950s and 1960s were party affairs. Candidates were subject to party people and platform. The party ran the campaigns and raised the money. I understood that role well; in 1952, as a state senator, I had been the manager of the Minnesota Republican statewide campaign. It was my job, and a considerable one, to maintain control of state campaign finances. Candidates never personally solicited money; the party and candidates' finance committees did that. I was very familiar with the routine. In 1946 I raised money for Ed Devitt's successful campaign for Congress. We had a budget of $30,000, and the party's money group thought that was extravagant. We said, "You haven't been winning. It costs money to win. You can lose cheap."

Thirty thousand dollars now is hardly a campaign budget for a state Senate seat. Even beyond inflation, the imperative of money in politics has become much more vast. I've always considered that an unfortunate development. Now, any person who can raise money can be a candidate. It requires no internship, no prior service, no preparation, no qualification. You just run. The parties served the nation better when candidates had to be known to the party to receive nomination. The screening that candidates were given under that system was more thorough.

When I ran for governor, it was very much as a party person. I had been active in party affairs for twenty-six years. Seeking the governorship was not just a personal decision. It was a volunteering of my effort to make the party strong, to build a strong platform, to build a strong ticket. If the party decided that I could represent it in the governorship, I was willing. That was the spirit in which I announced my candidacy in January 1960. It was a statement of willingness to run. The full text follows:

⏭ For several months I have been visiting various parts of the state with a sense of urgency about the 1960 election campaign. It is apparent to me that the people of Minnesota are dissatisfied with the present administration and are looking for new leadership.

Our people feel misled in reference to spending and taxing programs. They are agitated about present record levels of debt and tax levies. They dislike seeing weak administration of mental health, highway and other programs. There is no long-range plan for higher education. Most recently the fundamentals of law enforcement and constitutional protections have been put in jeopardy and rescued only by action of the Federal court.

To fill the leadership vacuum in our state with a Republican success in the 1960 elections, I have been urging the recruiting of a strong slate of candidates, the development of a constructive Republican program, the attraction of adequate resources for an effective campaign, and the necessity of an early start to do a thorough job of organization and communication.

An increasing number of people have urged me to become a candidate for governor, or at least let it be known that I would be available, so that they could organize volunteer efforts in my behalf. In the months ahead it will be my plan to cooperate with party officers and leaders to unify and strengthen the Republican Party in Minnesota, to aid in calling the present administration to a stern accounting for its record, to work on the constructive, distinctively Republican program I consider so essential, and to help win supporters to the Republican cause. If, in developing all the factors needed for Republican success in 1960, there is a decisive call from the people for me to be the Republican candidate for governor and, the party convention wishes to endorse me, I would make myself available. I feel a deep sense of gratitude to my family and my business associates for their cooperation in the implications of this statement. I would not become a candidate without the party's endorsement, and I will support the ticket the party chooses. I have strong convictions about citizenship responsibility, and if this is mine, I'm ready.

—January 5, 1960

THE BENEFITS OF BEING A HIGH-TAX STATE

Governor Orville Freeman, who died in March of 2003, was my adversary in the 1960 campaign. But he was also my friend and ally in enacting important welfare and education bills during the 1950s. Even in the closing days of the campaign, when I was speaking to a rally at the old Prom Ballroom in St. Paul, I did not attempt to rouse the audience with a personal attack on Freeman. I respected both him and my audience too much to make that kind of appeal for votes.

Rather, I made a case that I would make again in a statewide campaign today. People need quality services from government, and the way to provide them is through industrial development. Industrial development is built around education and investment in people, not tax cuts. Anyone who knows business knows that taxes are really not the issue that decides where firms locate. The crucial issue, after consideration of market, is the adequacy of the available workforce. An industry surrounding new development goes where people are trained and skilled in that development. The firms that choose low-tax states are those that can tolerate poor education because they rely on low-wage, unskilled labor. Desirable industries, those that pay high wages and seek to maximize the per-capita production of each employee, need the things that a high-tax state provides. They need a fine workforce of well-educated, healthy people who are attracted to a place because of its culture and amenities, not its cheapness.

Minnesota has enjoyed great success with a high-services strategy. When I ran for governor in 1960, personal income was below the national average, and population was declining. Not long afterward, the state's average income began to climb, until it reached fourth-highest in the nation in 2000. It's so sad that some people in my own Republican Party seem not to have learned the lesson that taxes do not harm the economy. They help it, by creating a better workforce and place to do business.

During my campaigns, I always called on Minnesotans to come and work together in harmony to build the economy. That would be a good slogan for the present: Come together to build the economy. Here's how I said it in 1960:

⏭ In our state campaign, we have some very practical issues. We must decide whether an administration that has been in for six years, as long as any in the history of our state, is so outstanding that it should be extended to an unprecedented fourth term, or whether new leadership can do better from here on. As we review the record, the evidence mounts that a change is imperative for the sake of our future well-being.

The people of Minnesota resent the 1958 deception when they were led to believe there would be no new taxes or revenue needed, only to have the re-elected governor submit an $84 million demand to the legislature. A bitter legislative session resulted and the seeds for further difficulties were sown.

The current school crisis is but one indication of financial mismanagement. People are concerned about the school crisis —alarmed to find the state cannot pay school aids on time because the administration was a party to using large amounts of school funds for other purposes. Some schools faced closing as a result and school districts throughout the state are pinched for funds and finding it necessary to borrow money and incur unbudgeted interest costs. As of now, the income tax school fund which had a balance of $38 million on June 30, 1955 is exhausted, $50 million of borrowing capacity has been used up, and $54 million dollars of state aid to school districts is due and unpaid.

The general revenue fund, the state's main checking account, which had a $1.5 million balance on June 30, 1955, was down to a $1.9 million deficit on June 30, 1960 and the state at times has had to borrow money to pay current bills and meet the payroll. The fact is that, high as your taxes are, your state administration is spending money faster than it is coming in.

In the October 17 issue of *U.S. News and World Report*, there was a table of state and local taxes per $1,000 of personal income. Minnesota ranked 8th among all the states and was $250 above the U.S. average. Our taxes are among the highest in the country. Our per capita income, on the other hand, is below the national average. It is also below the average of the Plains states around us. The plain and fully documented fact is that our per capita income is below the national average, our state and local governmental spending, far above the national average.

Our problem is twofold: First we must scrutinize all government operations and reduce costs, particularly administrative costs, wherever possible. This I will work on intensively. Secondly, if we are to support the programs we believe important, we simply must increase the earnings of our people, add to the numbers of our taxpayers, and expand the industrial tax base. This, the present administration fails to comprehend. Actually, the lag in our business development is a great area of weakness, and one reason for our governmental costs and taxes becoming such an individual burden.

Four of Minnesota's largest firms, national organizations with their home offices here, declined in production workers from 1954 to 1960 by 2,403. They increased office and research workers because of their home offices being here by 3,299. This then was a net increase in employment of 896 jobs, but these same four Minnesota firms increased production workers outside of Minnesota by 6,230 and office workers by 7,031. These firms have said they would like to expand in Minnesota, but conditions do not justify it. How in the world can we expect to bring new business to Minnesota when we discourage the growth of that which is already here?

During my legislative service, I was very much interested in strong educational programs, good support for our junior colleges, state colleges and university, adequate programs in the field of welfare, a really intensive treatment program in our mental hospitals and in all of the other services that are the proper state's responsibility, a complete facing up to the needs and meeting them well. This is still my feeling and will continue to be my dedication. But what concerns me is that if we do not have the economic development to provide the wherewithal to support these programs, they simply will not be sustained. The present administration does not deserve re-election, for it utterly fails to face the challenge of economic development.

I pledge myself to the most careful scrutiny of every budget and expenditure plan in state government. I have had experience in this both in the legislature and in private business, and my goal will be to produce the greatest value for every tax dollar expended while protecting the essential services needed by our people.

May I say also that we do not look for government to do everything for all people. It has always been my belief that the fundamental responsibility is with each family. I would do everything we can to strengthen family life and to bolster family responsibility. Likewise I believe we should recognize the great role of the church, and I will provide leadership in every way I can to encourage people to support the church of their choice. I have long been a supporter of the voluntary community agency in fields of welfare, youth activity and other programs. I believe strongly in the individual. As one evidence of our concern for every individual, it will be our plan as governor to set aside a specific time each week for open appointments in the governor's office where any citizen with a problem can come in and visit with his governor and secure his personal help without prior arrangement. We live in a complicated society and I have seen much evidence of the difficulty some people have with governmental procedures. I hope this will be one way to cut through some of the obstruction that frustrates people and let them at least have the satisfaction of coming in to see their governor and having a visit with him.

As I have traveled back and forth across the state many times in the past year, there is an obvious frustration of standing still, even going behind. Throughout Minnesota, progress is eluding great people who have the talent, the resources, and the desire to group our forces and get going. The single greatest issue in this campaign is the development of unity. To solve Minnesota's problems, we need a new administration that will marshal the people and resources to action. We need a governor who will work in a conciliatory way with the legislature to get important legislation that is needed. We must fight the formidable common enemy of division. We must bridge the gap that separates labor, management and government in the mining industry. We must avoid angry government that berates one group, or plays another group against a third. We cannot marshal our people and resources with such belligerence. We need everybody and we need everybody working together. Unity will marshal the great people and abundant resources of Minnesota. Unity will bring co-operative efforts of farmer and worker, of management and labor, of liberals and conservatives; it will produce jobs on the Range and in our rural communities; it will produce a healthy program of unrestricted progress. Unity is working together. This is what I propose for Minnesota. I invite you to join our efforts with your support, your work, your ideas and your vote.

—October 24, 1960

STATE BUDGETS: SELF-INDULGENCE IS NOT A VIRTUE

One of the roles a good political leader should assume is that of educator. That's the role I tried to play in 1961, as a governor who had concluded that the state should raise taxes. I recommended the establishment of a state surcharge on utility bills. As I spoke to Minnesota audiences trying to sell that unpopular idea, I took great care to explain the reasons for growth in state spending, and the need to meet growing needs with growing revenue.

People are wise. They make good decisions if they get the facts. But they are easily misled when somebody preaches that self-indulgence is a virtue. In a demagogic way, that is the message that politicians have been giving Americans in recent decades. Rather than explaining what government does, politicians often belittle it. They put the government not in the role of service provider, but in the role of competitor for people's money. The whole attitude between government and the governed becomes adversarial, not cooperative, as it should be.

Paying taxes is like going to a store. You don't go to a store with the purpose of spending money. You go to obtain something you need or want. That should be the approach to paying taxes. Taxes aren't a loss of money; they are the price of essential services. It's been an easy political game to promise tax cuts, and to make people feel sorry for themselves, when as a matter of fact, the taxes people pay are probably the best investment they make. They can be proud to pay the price, if it lifts the standard of social life in their community and state. People need to be educated about government budgets, so they understand that tax money goes to services they want, and that if they don't pay the price, they suffer.

I explained my budget proposal to the members of the Minnesota Newspaper Association a few weeks after the start of the 1961 legislative session. It was an extemporaneous speech that was recorded and later transcribed. I considered many members of my audience friends, so I also shared with them a glimpse of my life as governor, and paid tribute to my helpmate, then and always, Eleanor Johnson Andersen. Here is some of what I said:

⏭ I was very interested in your program. I saw something about a panel this afternoon, "Women Publishers and Working Wives of Newspaper Publishers." I couldn't help but think of my own working wife, as she most surely is on this new job we are sharing. After a full day on Wednesday, we drove to Princeton in the evening and attended a large meeting, spoke and shook hands with everybody within reach, and then came home. We got home after midnight; got up early yesterday morning; had an early breakfast meeting; on the go all day; left about 3:30 or 4 for Fairmont for a meeting last night to bring the word of encouragement to that citadel of liberalism down in that part of the state; spent a good deal of time shaking hands there afterward; got home well after midnight, and up again for an early news conference this morning. Mrs. Andersen has been right along all the way. She is truly a "working wife," and it is not only a wonderful thing, but also a truly great help. I appreciate it.

I have truly always enjoyed associations with newspaper people. I was thinking about it the other night at the Gridiron Banquet: "I am going to be a newspaper man some day myself." I really think that might someday come about. I want to thank you for the courtesies shown us last fall. As I look around the room, I can see a great many of you with whom I visited in your shops and offices around the state.

We enjoy the new job that is now ours. "Why does someone do this sort of thing?" someone asked me last night. Some people kind of feel sorry for you. No one has to feel sorry for us. We wanted this, and we worked awfully hard to obtain this opportunity, so we treasure it. When you wonder, "Why?," I think the best answer to that question is one given by Sir Edmund Hillary. He was asked, "Why do you want to climb Mount Everest? Why would anyone want to climb a mountain where so many had lost their lives?" He said, "It was there. I suppose one of the reasons why we do anything is simply the challenge." There are things to be done, and some people just like to pitch in and do them. It is the challenge of achievement that is probably the greatest motivation.

I thought I would discuss a little with you what we have been up to in the weeks that have gone by and to try to share with you our goal.

Of course, one of the first responsibilities is submitting a budget to the legislature, suggesting spending and then, also, suggesting revenue. As I have mentioned once or twice before, I remember so very well a few hours after the budget message, I saw the first newspaper reporting it and in bold, black type was the announcement "Andersen Submits Record High Budget—Proposes New Taxes." I think it would be clear, that wouldn't be the choice of anyone. It would be much more satisfying if you could see the headline, "Andersen Cuts the Budget—Calls for Reduced Taxes." It would be nice to be that kind of a hero! I would like to share just a few of the decisions that went into the spending side of the budget for the next two years.

Here was one: Two years ago the legislature outlined some formulas for state aid to education. They appropriated the money to pay those state aids, but they didn't appropriate enough money. The appropriation was short by $18 million of being enough to cover the aid provided in the formulas. So, in my budget for the next two years, if I didn't provide for any more children, if I didn't provide for any *increase* in the cost of service, if I just provided exactly the same as two years ago, I would be $18 million higher than two years ago. Right off the bat, before your feet are off the ground, you are $18 million higher than the budget of two years ago!

But we don't have the same number of pupils. We have 60,000 more pupil units. (A pupil unit, as you know, is a grade school child. A high school student is 1.5 units.) The average cost of a grade school child is $300 a year, times 60,000 more, equals $18 million more, or $36 million for the biennium. About 44 percent of that is state cost, so there is a whole batch more of millions of dollars on top of the $18 million already picked up. It seems you should make some recognition of higher costs. The legislature doesn't determine what education is going to cost. It determines what share is going to be borne by state aid, and what share will be placed on local property. The state's percentage had been in the area of 44 percent. I thought we should at least keep it the same, so I made a slight (I thought "slight" and some of the school districts think "slight") adjustment in the formula. The net result was that in education, there was a substantial increase over two years ago. To me, inevitable! To you, facing the same facts, just as inevitable. Some of you might have felt no increase in the state aid level would be required. Many of you might have felt it should be higher than the level that I recommended. In all of these decisions, there is room for individual differences of opinion.

When you turn to welfare, this is a big cost item. What do you do there? Well, the state has been building some new buildings to house some of the people we haven't had room for, particularly in the area of the mentally retarded. It is a great shock to a family to have a mentally retarded child born into the family. After some period of time of adjusting and keeping the child at home as long as possible, seeking out resources and possible local school programs, the time comes in many families when they feel they must commit the child to the state. So they do, only then to learn they might have to wait two or three years before the state can take custody, even after they take legal commitment.

This is because of the shortage, so we have been trying to catch up on this need, which still is in the area of 800 or 900 new beds. We were trying to do it while I was in the legislature. We are still trying to do it. As the new facilities become available, we simply need new personnel, of course. It is inevitable that if you build an additional hospital, you are going to need additional personnel. So that accounted for some increase.

The doctors made a request for drugs in our mental hospitals. I don't know who can presume to tell a doctor how much medicine he needs when he is treating sick people, and I don't know what kind of savings we want to make (and I know we want to make some) but I can't feel that we should tell doctors that they are asking for too much medicine. There is only one thing you can do with medicine -- give it to people who are sick—and I don't think doctors, generally, would give more than a patient needed. I felt it necessary and advisable to recommend the full amount of the drugs requested by the doctors. This involved a $500,000 or $600,000 increase.

The amazing thing with a budget of these dimensions is that relatively small items on an individual basis expand to large amounts of money on a statewide basis. One example of this: We are currently spending in our mental hospitals 63 cents a day per patient for food. That isn't quite as bad as it sounds, because it is supplemented by surplus commodities that come to us free. It is supplemented by produce raised on the farms. It should be considered in the context of the way the state buys. Still, it is 63 cents a day per patient. The recommendation was made that this be increased by two cents a day. Now, I don't know who would want to presume to deny a patient in a mental hospital two cents a day more for food. Would you? I didn't feel that I should! So I recommended it. But two cents a day—two pennies a day—for food in our mental hospitals amounts to a $248,000 increase in the budget. These are the kinds of questions you must face up to, and they are hard to say "No" to.

One other in this area that was a pretty substantial item: our state employees had not had a change in their pay rates for four years. The Civil Service Board had made a study of over 500 firms covering thousands of employees, to see where our state employees stood relative to the same jobs in private employment. They found them to be behind, and they recommended some adjustments. They are not huge raises by any means. The state employees, while grateful for any recognition, bring out this fact: The study was made nearly a year ago. If adopted by the legislature, it wouldn't become operative for at least six months, and maybe not for a year. By the time they are receiving the increase now under consideration, based on a previous study, they are lagging two years behind private employment already. While looking for places to reduce the number of employees, I believe that employees are good employees when they are adequately paid, so I recommended this item. It is a small item in individual jobs, but

$9.6 million in the total budget for the biennium. These are the tough decisions!

It has been said, "How does this face up with what you were talking about during the campaign of fiscal responsibility? Isn't this kind of irresponsible, to come up with a budget much higher than before?" To me, what "fiscal responsibility" is, is facing up to the spending with taxing. "Fiscal irresponsibility" to me is thinking you can spend without taxing, or actually spending more than you are taking in, or leading people to believe you can have services that someone off yonder with the ability to pay will pay for. That, to me, is where the irresponsibility comes in. I believe the level of spending is for the people to determine with all the facts before them, and the price tag right alongside of the service. There is where you can perform a great function—informing the people what the service is, its desirability, what the cost is, and then through this interchange in development of public opinion, get a proper balance. Where government spending gets out of line is where the price tag isn't closely enough identified with the service and the taxpayer's individual identity with the cost not sufficiently made clear.

We are trying, and you can do a great service, too, to simply get the facts before our people. I think we just must understand that the governmental activity now is so broad, reaches so many of the lives of our people, that we all need to be involved, and so help me, I think we should be proud to be involved. I don't think we need to feel sorry for ourselves for necessary expenditures, for good services that are prudently administered. We live in a rich and wonderful country. Our people are blessed beyond that of the peoples of other countries. Very little has been required of our people in the way of over-all sacrifice. Individual families have suffered, that is true, but we are a richly blessed and wonderful country, and we have a great responsibility in this world. I don't think we should feel so sorry for ourselves for an $1.80 a month average contribution [Andersen's tax proposal] to get our financial house in order, to get rid of the deficiencies and the debts, and to begin to provide the essential services we should.

—February 17, 1961

HIGHWAY SAFETY

Highway safety was a major concern in Minnesota in the 1950s and 1960s, and for good reason. Most of the highways in those years had only two lanes. They were an abomination. People were driving toward each other just a few feet apart, in opposite directions, at high speeds. In wintry weather, the slightest slip or skidding would put one in the path of an oncoming vehicle. Those two-lane roads had been designed decades earlier, when cars were fewer in number and less powerful. The automobiles of the 1950s were formidable machines, but they lacked seat belts, air bags, padded interiors and other safety features that are now standard. What's more, speed limits on state roads in the metro area were higher than today. The result by 1960 was an annual highway death toll of more than 700 Minnesotans—much higher than today's toll in terms of deaths per 1,000 miles driven.

We are so fortunate today that investments were made in the 1960s and 1970s to transform our most heavily traveled highways into divided, four-or-more lane expressways. By and large, the two-lane highways that remain today are in rural areas, and bear relatively little traffic. An issue I faced as governor was whether to build the first four-lane highways in Greater Minnesota, where we could show the most mileage for the money, or give priority to the metropolitan area, where traffic snarls were a problem but costs per mile were enormous. We decided that the metropolitan area had the greater need, so we put the priority there. It's clear today that we made the right decision.

There's a lesson for today in what we did then. We made a big investment in infrastructure that would serve Minnesota for decades to come. We still enjoy the benefit of those investments, and will far into the future. But in the 1990s, Minnesota's investment in its transportation system—roads, bridges, rail, buses, airfields—did not keep pace with the investments of most states. Traffic congestion has become a huge problem in the Twin Cities, and the safety of those crowded highways is again an issue. The legislature has failed even to appropriate the matching funds needed to leverage a grant of federal dollars for metro transit. The state's unwillingness to invest in its transportation infrastructure today will inconvenience and endanger its citizens far into the future. Minnesota leaders have to make transportation investment a priority.

When we were building the four-lane highway system in the metro area, the chief of the highway department said, "We're not going to accomplish very much. The volume of traffic is growing faster than our ability to build highways. There's going to have to be a different approach, a different solution, some kind of public transportation system that the people will accept and use." How wise he was! It is increasingly clear that it is impossible for the state to provide all the highways needed for everybody to be personal chauffeurs. More mass transit must be made available in the metro area.

I delivered a special message to the legislature in 1961 on traffic safety. Here is some of what I said:

⏭ Every member of this legislature knows that the people of our state want our laws relating to traffic safety strengthened. No subject has brought more mail. A large number of bills have been introduced. This interest is easy to understand in the face of a record toll of lives on our highways in 1960, and 1961 fatalities running even higher than a year ago. It is imperative that we focus attention on the most essential measures, and press for immediate action to assure enactment of a sound program on which our people insist.

I respectfully urge you to act promptly and favorably on bills that provide for implied consent for blood-alcohol testing of those suspected of driving under the influence of alcohol; a driver education requirement for the granting of licenses to those under age eighteen; required vision examinations upon drivers' license renewal;

an increase in highway patrol strength; stiffer penalties for driving without a license; and standard speed limits on all state highways.

There are additional proposals also worthy of your favorable action that would contribute much to an effective program. These are the adoption of a uniform traffic tag, the requirement of tested safety devices such as seat belts, special penalties for aggravated speeding offenses, and the use of unmarked patrol cars.

To supplement your efforts in making more effective laws available, we in the executive branch will stress strict enforcement; we will urge municipal judges to effectively use the penalties provided; and we will generate programs of safety education, and coordinate all agencies relating to traffic safety in the most effective way we can devise.

I am convinced that the citizens of Minnesota are in favor of these laws designed to save property, pain and lives. This conviction is based on the many messages that have come to my office from people all over our state. We have tabulated more than 1,700 letters that expressed a definite stand on specific issues. We found that 82 percent favored implied consent; 57 percent favored unmarked patrol cars; 95 percent favored driver education for all persons under eighteen; 60 percent favored examination for all drivers upon license; 88 percent favored increase in highway patrol strength, and 88 percent favored stiffer penalties for drivers' license violations.

All of these messages indicate a great public concern for reducing traffic accidents. They expect action, for even as we deliberate these matters, the rate of traffic fatalities is increasing. With your cooperation we will mount an offensive against this frightful slaughter, and insist on effective results.

—March 23, 1961

WHAT ROLE GOVERNMENT? STRIKING A BALANCE

I have often defended government against uninformed claims that it is wasteful, or that its work is insignificant. But I am still a Republican. I believe government's role should be limited. People need to do what they can for themselves. They should be helped to be self-supporting, rather than be supported, except when self-help is an impossibility. Government must respect the rights and liberties of the individual. But it should do things for people that they cannot do, or cannot do as well, for themselves.

A good balance between personal responsibility, private sector and community responsibility, and government is what is needed. It takes everybody working efficiently to put together all the elements of a happy society. It also takes citizen vigilance and participation in government.

That participation extends to the payment of taxes. I have always favored graduated taxes, or progressive taxes, with those who can afford to do so paying more. Progressive taxation is not a matter of "soaking the rich." It's a matter of a fair balance between those of substantial means and those less fortunate. It should be a matter of satisfaction to those who have done well within the American system to be able to help make the system work for others. But I have also argued that everyone should pay some tax, so that every person has a vested interest in the actions of government. There should be no non-payer of taxes among the American citizenry. Everybody benefits from government, and everybody can contribute something to it.

I tried to describe what I believed was a desirable balance between the individual and government when I spoke to the Carleton College Republican Club in 1959. It was a time of concern about the rapid growth of the scope of the federal government. My theme was "challenging opportunities."

⏭ As our country has grown in numbers, social problems have become more complex, and we have tended to look to government for more of the answers. It has always been my feeling that government should assume the residual jobs that other agencies in our society either cannot do or fail to do. Anything that can be done to strengthen the family to carry its responsibilities should be done. I would hope that the future would show the churches carrying a greater share of the social services load than they now carry, much good work as they do. Where the family and the churches fall short, I would hope volunteer local community agencies would become stronger. In all of these areas, we strengthen individuals as well as obtaining aid for those who need it or service for those who can benefit from it. Many of these values are lost when government becomes the agency for social service.

With this said, however, we then turn to the role the government must play where the needs are not met otherwise. In our country, and under our form of government, the individual is all-important. We respect his freedom, his divinity, and his right to life, liberty and the pursuit of happiness. In fact, the people who founded our government retained the sovereignty in the people, and yielded to the government only sufficient powers to carry on functions that the people could not discharge individually. Therefore, in looking for challenging opportunities, we first might well direct our attention to how the individual is prospering in our country and in our state.

The answer is a favorable one on an over-all basis. By whatever statistical comparisons one would use, the individual Minnesotan is prosperous, healthy, has great material comfort, has fine outlets for his abilities, opportunities for training, and his lot in life is one to make it desired by most of the peoples of the world. This is on an average basis.

We must recognize that it is far less true for some than for others. Where it is less true because of bias or prejudice toward any of our people, then it is a challenging opportunity. We must admit that even in Minnesota, there is less opportunity for Negroes than for people of the white race. Where prejudice and restrictions remain, they should be eliminated. The government can do its share by establishing standards and declaring principles. This it did in passing the Fair Employment Practices Act, of which I was proud to be a sponsor in the state Senate. It is eliminating discrimination in employment, and is not any great burden on management. We must recognize that in some of these areas the practical application is not the whole thing; the psychological application is also important. The Fair Employment Bill meant a great deal to some of our minority groups because it established and declared a principle of our society. Similar action is needed in the field of housing to eliminate discrimination. We must lend our support to school integration on an understanding and sympathetic but persistent basis.

One minority problem in Minnesota goes begging for an answer, and that is of our Indian citizens. There is no more challenging opportunity in Minnesota today than that of providing opportunity and rehabilitation to our Indian population.

Minnesota has another challenging opportunity that is common to all of the states and that is in relation to our senior citizens. The situation is particularly compelling to this generation. Our people are living longer, which means we will have a greater percentage of seniors in our population. The people who are now reaching the age of sixty-five were in their forties during the depression of the 1930s. At the time when they should have been at the peak of their earning power and saving power, they were struggling to make ends meet. Such savings as they could accumulate have been eroded by inflation. Very few people over sixty-five today are without financial problems of some kind or other.

Honoring its senior citizens is a benchmark of any civilization and has been an exhortation to every people from the earliest biblical times. We are going to need a new concept of how long people can work, we are going to need interim programs of work and retirement, we are going to need more in the way of housing accommodations, either private or voluntary, to meet the challenge of providing happy years for our fathers and mothers. This should be done on a family, church or community basis, but the residual problem will become that of state government, and should be met.

With all our effort to encourage the family, the church, local volunteer agencies and county and municipal governments, it is going to be exceedingly difficult to restrain the growth of state and federal government. Many situations simply will demand service by state and federal governments in areas not even now practiced. Two areas become very challenging, then, in relation to government and its activities: one relates to efficiency, the other, to support.

In the area of efficiency, Minnesota has many opportunities. There have been numerous studies indicating many areas of improvement. I believe the most fundamental thing the people of Minnesota could do to bring about governmental efficiency would be to have a constitutional convention to revise our state constitution. Most of the problems that face the present legislature and become the subject of such wrangling, relating to organization in the executive branch of the government, operation of the legislature itself, reapportionment, tax reform, and many, many others, all relate to constitutional revision. I have always felt that the people could be depended upon to select delegates for a constitutional convention who would be true to their trust, would do a workmanlike job of retaining the best of our constitution, and revising and improving where needed, so that the people would be justified in approving the work when it was done. If they did not, there is the safeguard of disapproval. This is but one challenging opportunity, but I hope it will soon be accomplished.

In the area of support for government, we have had a generation or more of political preaching intended to give the impression that we could have many governmental services, for which someone else would pay. This has been part of the reason for the vast growth of the federal government. The cost of services has been more removed from individual understanding and consciousness.

The challenging opportunity is to place government on a higher plane of acceptance and respect, and support the people who are in it in a manner worthy of the job they are doing. I mean schoolteachers, civil servants, social workers, and all who are in public employ. Then sell the people on the idea that the services are important, they are a great benefit to all, and that all should participate directly, specifically and willingly in their support, on a basis of services rendered as well as ability to pay. This means a broader base of tax participation in Minnesota than we have now.

A great deal is said about tax reform as a basis for attracting industry. I believe a more fundamental reason for tax reform in Minnesota is that public services are important. They are entitled to respect and support. The services are now so broadly needed that everyone will have to be directly supporting them if they are to be properly maintained. The basis of "ability to pay" has been used to a point where too many people feel that it is only others who are able to pay. Nearly everyone is now able to pay something directly to the cost of these services, and it is in their own best interest that they do so.

This leads me to the final challenging opportunity, which is that of individual responsibility in the public interest. To an alarming degree our government has become one of rival pressure groups. In our legislature one can see the action of contending forces. Individual groups, of whatever kind, are before the legislature pressing for one kind of legislation or another, of particular interest to their own group. Many of them, I suppose most of them, consider themselves as working in the public interest, but in many cases, the public interest is secondary to the special interest of the group involved. There are cases, also, where the special interest is in direct conflict with the public interest.

The only solution is citizen awareness, and a citizen sense of responsibility. As citizens, there is a great challenge to know more about our government, to follow its activities, to let our interests be known. Legislatures and other representative bodies are responsive to the public will. If the public is indifferent, however, then almost anything can happen. As it has been said, the sure way for evil to prevail is for the good people to do nothing.

—April 29, 1959

THE FEDERAL ROLE

Minnesota was ill-prepared for the economic downturn that began in 2001. Because of large tax reductions and rebates in the 1990s, the state slipped quickly into serious financial trouble. A new governor and legislators are telling Minnesotans that the solution is to cut back on government. What grieves me is that they think they are doing government a service; that it has become too costly and inefficient, and that the people working in it are not sufficiently ambitious and dedicated.

All this is contrary to my experience. In Minnesota, public service is well rendered. Sometimes it's said that we have to learn to live within our means. Our means are adequate to our vision. If we want to have a fine state, we're going to have to pay more than those who have less ambition for their state. If they care only for some of their state's people, they can have low-cost government. We want opportunity for everyone, and a decent life for everyone. That costs money, but it's a good investment, one that has proven its worth over time.

The federal government has been Minnesota's partner in many endeavors—transportation, higher education, health care for the poor and more. But so often, the federal government has mandated programs that go under-funded. The special education program was a particular interest of mine. I sponsored the bill that launched the state special education program in 1957. When the federal government took it on in about 1970, they promised to pay 40 percent of the cost. They've never paid more than 15 percent. This is a shortcoming that applies to many federal activities.

It's a problem whose solution goes back, as so many problems in a democracy do, to the need for public awareness and participation. The people can get whatever they want.

Congress is constantly polling to see what people think. If people fail to play their rightful role in self-governance, they will not be likely to get what they deserve from federal and state government. Individual participation in government, in staying informed, in communicating with elected officials, in working in one's political party, and in voting—that is the key.

In the 1960s, the federal government's role was an issue as many of the nation's large cities experienced the trauma of race-related violence. The States' Urban Action Center, a non-profit, non-partisan group, was formed to assist states and governors in solving the underlying problems that provoked racial unrest, and to speak for those states to the federal government. Here is some of what I said to the center's Assembly on Intergovernmental Cooperation about federal versus state obligations in 1967:

⏭ The States' Urban Action Center has been created with the idea that the government should provide certain services, should perform certain regulatory activities, and should guarantee basic liberties. The only question is which government—state or national. Obviously, some programs, such as Social Security, and certain regulatory activities, such as the regulations of interstate transportation and of the use of television channels, are national in character and fall under the auspices of the national government.

In other matters, however, it is not the interstate nature of the problem that has brought in the national government. The national government got into hospital construction because state and local governments had neglected hospitals. The national government came to the general support of education because states were not spending enough to reach goals most American citizens considered important to achieve. The national government became involved in slum clearance because the state and local governments didn't become involved, or at least didn't do so sufficiently.

There is evidence today, however, that the states are attempting with new vigor to reform themselves. Today, over half the states are conducting constitutional or administrative revisions, and study commissions in many other states are preparing recommendations. In the 1966 election alone, voters in fourteen states considered amendments to reorganize the legislature; in eight states, they voted on changes in the executive branch; in thirteen states, on judicial changes; in four states, on other basic constitutional amendments; and in eleven states, on revisions of the relations between state and local governments. Not all efforts toward reform were successful, nor were they all in the same direction, but an impulse towards improvement of state government is clearly present.

One of the most valuable contributions states have made is that of acting as "the laboratories of democracy." Supreme Court Justice Louis Brandeis wrote: "It is one of the happy incidents of the federal system that a single courageous state may, if its citizens choose, serve as a laboratory to try novel social and economic experiments without risk to the rest of the country." Examples of states acting as laboratories for programs of interest to the rest of the country are many. New York State's attack on water pollution is one example. The 1966 Kentucky civil rights bill is another. Every recommendation now carried forward by the Federal Highway Safety Program has come from the states. Areas such as prisoner rehabilitation, mental health, and education owe a great deal to the experimentation of various states.

We all must agree that the urban crisis has posed a challenge to all governmental leadership. The States Urban Action Center joins with the governors to provide leadership and programs for action. We truly look forward to serving the states as they work in their own imaginative ways toward meaningful solutions.

—December 14, 1967

NEVER DONE

Since its founding after Vice President Hubert Humphrey's death in 1978, the Humphrey Institute at the University of Minnesota has been something of a haven for Democrats. Not many Republicans have been active thereabouts. Therefore, I went in May 2003 a little as a foreign visitor, but the crowds were very warm and enthusiastic, both at the Humphrey Institute Leadership Awards banquet and the Freeman Forum that month. On both occasions, I soon felt much at home.

When I spoke on May 1, as I received one of four Humphrey Institute Public Leadership Awards, I got caught up in the stories told by a young Hmong leader and a leader in the field of deafness who were also honored that night. I included them in my remarks because of the fine examples of citizenship they provide. I was also pleased to be honored along with former Vice President Walter Mondale.

I commented about the debate over balancing the state budget that was just then at its high point in the legislature. I disagreed with the Republicans who were trying to balance the budget exclusively with spending cuts, doing damage to education and health care and other needed services in the process. I favored a state tax increase instead. The response from the crowd was as if they had been waiting to hear something of that kind from me. The audience just exploded in approval.

On May 12, I was back at the Humphrey Institute with three other former governors on a panel as part of the Freeman Forum. It was an occasion devoted to discussion of the meaning of consensus and the common good in Minnesota life, dedicated to the DFL governor whom I succeeded in office, Orville Freeman. I had great respect and fondness for him and his wife Jane. It was Jane's invitation that brought me to the panel, which also included Republicans Al Quie and Arne Carlson, and DFLer Wendell Anderson. Lori Sturdevant, this book's editor, was our moderator.

The four governors made headlines that day as we unanimously called for a state tax increase to soften the budget cuts being contemplated by Governor Tim Pawlenty and the 2003 legislature. Our argument did not prevail at the Capitol. But it gave encouragement to those who agreed with us. As I told them that day, they need to take their fight into political process, to precinct caucuses and party conventions, if they hope to eventually carry the day.

Here is some of what I said at the Humphrey Institute Public Leadership Award presentation:

⏭ I'm overwhelmed by the spirit of the people we've been hearing from—the spirit of love, the spirit of friendship, the spirit of equality, the spirit of freedom. I was so impressed with Pakou Hang and her work, and the Hmong clans who now live among us. They are bringing so much vitality, interest and desire. They are like the immigrants of old, who come not to take something away, but to bring something here. I just love them. I met state Senator Mee Moua. I just loved her bumper sticker: "Vote for Mee."

[About fellow award recipient Roberta Cordano, a leader in education for the deaf,] it reminds me of the early work we did in 1955. We had an interim commission on the problems of, we called them, handicapped children. We soon learned to call them exceptional children, because that included the gifted, and the gifted children were the most neglected of all children with exceptionality. The session of 1957 approved every recommendation of that interim study commission, and put Minnesota in the vanguard of the states in care and concern for every educable child, and the training of every child to the extent of his or her ability.

There have been mighty works of progress. But the work is never done. It's just never done. We are at a crucial time in our state and in our nation. Organizations like the Humphrey Institute need to do all they can to alert people to citizenship. We need our leaders, but we need followers who are informed and concerned and caring.

Public works take a long time. There are times that are very discouraging. You have to know that sometimes, when you undertake a project, it is going to be years in completion. We undertook to get a national park for Minnesota. It took ten years of intensive effort to get it authorized by Congress. It took another ten years to get land exchange with the state, and other necessary provisions, so that Congress could establish it. Then it took seven years more to get the money to build a building that made it usable and accessible to people. I remember being at the dedication of the visitor's center in 1987, and thinking about how it had been twenty-seven years in the making. It takes a long time.

You have to challenge. I loved the spirit of those who spoke tonight. They're aggressive. You have to challenge. I was going to challenge the statement of the chairman of the Republican Party on the Almanac [Twin Cities Public Television] show last Friday night, when he was talking about raising taxes as withdrawing money from the economy. Taxes don't withdraw money from the economy; they put money into the economy. [The crowd cheered.] I'd better quit, or I'll take some notion of running for something.

—May 1, 2003

I elaborated on the tax theme eleven days later at the Freeman Forum. Here are excerpts:

⏭ One thing that all governors learn is that you don't sell taxes. Taxes don't sell; program does. One time in St. Anthony Park, we polled the neighborhood as to how many people favored a youth center in Langford Park. About 93 percent of the people said they favored it. Then we asked if they would be willing to have a slight addition made to their property tax assessment, to cover the cost of it, and 95 percent said no.

There was one issue [in the 1950s and 1960s] that has application today. Minnesota was in the highest rank, relatively, of state taxes paid. There was some concern, as there always is, about being a high tax state. Yet during that time, Minnesota went from being below the national average in per capita income to being above the national average in per capita income. At that time, it went from being an out-migration state to an in-migration state. It changed from being a state of declining population to being a state of increasing population. The Minnesotans of that period accepted high taxes.

Someone said the other day that to tax now would be taking money out of the economy. To me, taxes put money into the economy, into essential public services, into education, into culture, parks and highways. It is unfortunate that a pledge was made to resolve the [state budget] deficit without tax increases. They might better be called revenue adjustments. The people of Minnesota want the kind of state we have had. They should let that be known.

There's a great deal of activity at the legislative session right now. People are meeting on the steps of the Capitol. But the decisions are not made at the Capitol during the legislative session. They are made at the precinct caucuses of each party. They are made during the campaign, when pledges are sought from candidates. To spend a lot of money and effort and time at the legislative session is not nearly as rewarding as getting into the system where the decisions are made, and participating in precinct caucuses and platform building.

Minnesota is a special state. We have wonderful public services. We kind of swallow hard on the taxes, but we wouldn't have it any other way. I hope we don't take too long getting away from it.

—May 12, 2003

II. SOCIAL JUSTICE

ATTACKING THE ROOTS OF DISCRIMINATION

Americans have made a great deal of progress in the last forty years in rooting out and eliminating discrimination against people because of their race, religion or ethnic origin. But discrimination is a malady of the human personality, and change comes slowly in that realm. An immense amount of work still needs to be done.

We tend to treat the symptoms of discrimination, rather than addressing the real disease. For example, if someone violates a Jewish Synagogue, society's response is to punish that person, rather than to figure out what has caused the hatred that person feels and to try to correct or eliminate it. Punitive measures by themselves fall short. In so many cases of difficulty, poverty, depravation, discrimination, lack of education, or lack of equality generate prejudice and hatred in people. People who commit hate crimes should be sentenced to serve the communities they have violated, and allowed to learn through education and exposure to overcome their prejudice. I'm a believer in restorative justice, which puts offenders into situations in which they not only pay for their crimes but also have an opportunity to reform the negative attitudes that were behind their actions.

If anything, American society has become more materialistic in the last four decades, and that has worked to keep discrimination alive. Poverty has always bred resentment. But in a society that equates the acquisition of goods with the enjoyment of life, widespread poverty adds to the sense of oppression that racial minorities have felt because of overt discrimination. We would do better to foster and give importance to those intangible things that can be shared without discrimination, instead of overvaluing the acquisition of material things that are limited in supply.

To the extent that there has been progress in defeating discrimination, I believe it has come in large measure because of education. Black and white Americans in large numbers began to be educated together in the last half of the twentieth century. Public schools have lifted up racial equality as a desirable national goal. Many more people of color, especially women, are getting college educations than ever before. That is reason for hope.

A word about the setting for this speech: It was given at the Informal Club, a venerable organization in St. Paul made up of business and professional people who put on informational programs from and for their own membership. One of the understandings was that a person would never be held to account elsewhere for what he said at the Informal Club. "Off the record" was the rule. I am violating that rule by publishing excerpts of this 1963 speech, a breach for which I hope my fellow members will forgive me.

I also hope the reader will forgive references to African Americans as Negroes, and the omission of other racial minorities. This speech's language and focus reflect its context, the burgeoning civil rights movement of the early 1960s. Were I to speak on this topic today, I would choose more inclusive language.

⏭ I have become increasingly impressed with the need for studying the sources of prejudice and discrimination in the minds of those who discriminate. Winning school, public accommodation and employment equality for the Negro will correct a grievous situation. Finding and rooting out the sources of prejudice and discrimination in the minds of the possessed would be a far greater accomplishment, for it would solve the overall problem of which the current battle for Negro rights is but one evidence.

At the close of World War II, before the fate of Adolph Hitler had been established, a group of English students were asked to write an answer to the question, "What shall we do with Hitler?" A Negro girl wrote a very brief answer. "Dress him up in a Negro skin and drop him anywhere in the United States for the remainder of his days," she said. This young lady could imagine no severer penalty than a life under the scourge of prejudice and discrimination, and she apparently felt it existed everywhere in our country.

For many months, matters relating to civil rights have dominated our news. Many of our people, previously relatively unaware of civil rights problems, have been concerned, disturbed, even horrified at events in Mississippi, Alabama, Georgia and other southern states. Pollsters have been busy measuring public reaction, and politicians have been no less occupied in evaluating impact on future elections. Most persons consider themselves tolerant, understanding people, wishing nothing but good for others, and generally favoring equal opportunity for all. Nevertheless, as the Negroes and their friends have been fighting to put an end to discrimination, a large and increasing percentage of American people are indicating that they feel the situation is "getting out of hand," that Negro sympathizers are going at it "too hard," or that corrective measures are "too extreme." In other words, they fear we are moving too rapidly toward a goal we profess to believe desirable. The plain fact is that the events and trends of recent months reveal that racial and other group prejudices exist in substantial proportions throughout our society and in all parts of our country.

Psychologists look upon discrimination as the manifestation of prejudice arising from conflict between groups. The word prejudice is from the Latin prejudicium, which means "a preceding judgment." In ancient Rome, it referred to a judicial pre-trial examination to determine the social status of litigants. In Rome, at that time, what one could do through the courts depended on one's position in the class system. The desire for group distinctions was implemented legally. Nazi Germany came around to all sorts of legal restrictions on Jews, and ultimately their extermination. We in the United States still legalize prejudice and discrimination in many ways.

Why do people have prejudice? Why do they discriminate against others on an irrational group basis? Is there a common denominator that would be a clue to solution of our knottiest social problem? Interesting studies have been made of the personality structure found among prejudiced people. In conducting such tests people would be given a list of ethnic groups and then given opportunity to express reaction to each group as whether one would like members, as citizens, neighbors in a community, fellow members of a club, diners at a public restaurant, members of a family through marriage and so on.

It has been clearly determined that people who tend to discriminate do so generally and broadly, and those who are tolerant in one relationship are understanding in their general outlook. In other words people have not been led to discriminate by the actions or circumstances of some particular group, but rather have an inward condition that makes them subject to prejudice against many groups.

The most telling study was by Eugene and Ruth Hartley, who devised a test involving thirty ethnic groups. Thirty-two were actual and three fictitious, the Damieans, the Pirenians and the Wallonians.

The results clearly demonstrated that people who felt prejudice toward Negroes also felt it toward many other easily identifiable minority groups. What's more, they didn't think much of the Damieans, Pirenians and Wallonians either! Clearly their attitudes were not based on facts or allegations relating to particular groups, but rather were expressions of a condition within themselves.

The Hartleys pursued their studies to determine the personality structure of prejudiced people. They found that a relatively tolerant personality was likely to exhibit a combination of the following characteristics: a strong desire for personal autonomy associated with a lack of need for dominance of others, a strong need for friendliness, fear of competition, a tendency to placate others, stronger than average interest in current events and ideas about bettering society, valuing personal achievement in vocations, dislike of violence, able to appreciate the contributions of others, conscious of feelings that people tend to be more or less alike, and possessed of a nurturing rather than a dominant attitude toward those younger.

By contrast, the relatively intolerant person displayed an unwillingness to accept responsibility, a preference for association in social groups rather than "serious" groups such as political parties, absorption with pleasure activities, a conscious conflict between work and play, emotionality rather than rationality and extreme egocentrism. He is relatively uncreative, apparently unable to deal with anxieties except by fleeing from them. Further, those who had the most prejudice seemed to be the people most insecure, plagued with a variety of fears, concerned about losing their jobs, wondering if they will succeed, uncertain about their status in society, people frustrated in one way or another. They use the Negro, Catholic, Mexican, or some other group as the target for their frustration.

Does harboring prejudice help those scared and frustrated people? Dr. Hortense Powdermaker, professor of anthropology, Queens College, New York City, says quite the contrary. "It acts as a blinder and prevents them from seeing the real cause of their insecurity, and from doing anything realistic about it. Instead they pick out some group to be the scapegoat, and the real situation responsible for their insecurity is left unchanged.

"Hence, prejudice prevents people from solving their difficulties. Also, prejudice warps the personality of the one holding it. Hate is destructive and uses up a lot of energy. If energy is used in hating Jews, or Negroes or Catholics, there is not much left for creative and constructive work. The prejudiced person becomes small and mean, and the kindlier and cooperative side of his nature becomes dwarfed. In time, his whole nature may become affected and all his human relationships suffer. It is impossible for him to get along with a wide variety of people or to mix well with anyone who is different from himself. This is not conducive to success."

It becomes evident that we have a major job of personality development with people harboring severe feelings of frustration, resentment and prejudice. How can we eliminate the deep-seated causes of prejudice, and how can we encourage the kind of mental outlook that tends to understanding and acceptance? This is the big practical problem.

In seeking causes for insecurity, frustration, and disappointment—the fertile soil for prejudice—we are led to look at the values considered important by the society in which the individual lives. People act in one way in orienting to values which can be shared by everyone, which are not scarce in the sense that one individual's possession will inhibit another's enjoyment. Religious experience is a conspicuous example, love of music, literature, ideas and conversation are others. One's enjoyment does not deny another. There is enough for all. Sharing with others enhances one person's satisfaction and enjoyment of such values.

People act differently in orientation to scarce, divisible and divisive values. Material goods are limited and divisible. For some to have more to achieve success usually means others must have less. Tensions develop during the struggle of acquisition. Prestige status becomes meaningful in terms of ranking within the system. For some to be high requires that others must be low. In a society where great emphasis is placed on material success, any group of generally low economic status that is seeking to gain ground can expect the prejudice and discrimination of individuals or groups feeling threatened in personal prestige or economic success.

Every society has to work out some equilibrium of value judgment and relative emphasis on tangible values versus the intangible. In America we have tended to place a very great emphasis upon competition for the so-called distributive values. At the same time we have a relatively low development of the shared non-divisible values. We established a government designed to free the individual, but have developed social and spiritual values that inhibit the fluidity of society essential to individual contentment. Thus we foster the very tensions that produce prejudice and discrimination. Trouble will continue to break out in one form or another until fundamental adjustments are made.

The nature of a solution suggests itself, and I will spell it out in general terms only. There must be conscious efforts to shift our emphasis from distributive and limited supply values to those in which one may share without denial to others. Is it too much to hope that we could get more emphasis on sharing and less on acquiring? Further, we must do a better job of distributing the gain produced by labor, so as to eliminate poverty, provide better housing, improve medical care, education and motivation among our under-privileged.

We must eliminate prejudice-building instruction of our children. We should develop cultural understanding by teaching scientific information about races and cultures, emphasizing the potential equality of races but the great variability within each group. We should increase contacts between groups, and let people learn that in many parts of the world, there is not the discrimination we take for granted.

I favor every kind of effort to achieve equality and opportunity for every person. I submit that a major part of the problem is personality disorder in the people doing the discriminating. Correcting that disorder is where massive efforts must be made.

—November 4, 1963

WOMEN OF UNDERSTANDING

Perhaps the most profound change in American life I have witnessed has been the change in the role of women. When I was a young adult in the 1930s, perhaps a quarter of all women worked outside the home. Today, Minnesota leads the nation with more than 70 percent of adult women in the workforce. That change came on strong in the 1970s, when the movement for women's equality under the law was most active. But some women were working on raising male consciousness of women's rights long before that, and one of them, working on me, was Eleanor Johnson Andersen.

Eleanor often reminded me to acknowledge and include women in my public remarks. Every time I'd mention men, she would want to be sure I meant women too. It was her influence that led me to occasionally substitute the word "woman" rather than "man" in referring generically to humankind, in order to school myself in gender equality. That is what I did when I spoke to the Altrusa Club in 1950.

Altrusa was a women's service club, much like Rotary and Kiwanis, which were exclusively male in those years. When those clubs opened to women, and when women went to work, and no longer had time for a lot of meetings and club work, organizations like Altrusa declined. Much has been gained through that change, but something has been lost as well.

It still takes enormous effort for a woman to rise to a position of direction in corporate America. Most women are still in secondary positions in the workplace, and as a result, they have little control of their time. Not many of them are employers and managers, able to take part in service-club work, go to conventions, travel, play golf and the like on company time and at company expense. What's more, too few corporations make a priority of service to the community, and encourage their employees, male or female, to be active in service clubs. Changing the culture of the workplace to better reflect women's values and enable women to participate in community service is unfinished business for the women's movement, and is something I would encourage.

Here is some of what I said to the Altrusa Club:

⏭ It is customary to use the word "man" in a generic sense to mean men and women. To even things up a bit, we would like to use the word "woman" meaning men and women.

To aid her in making her way in the physical world, natural woman is endowed with five senses—sight, hearing, taste, smell and touch. Any hereditary or accidental lack of any of these five senses is a great handicap to an individual. It seems that the woman of understanding needs five additional senses—five social senses—to aid her in living significantly in the social world. We might name these a sense of history, a sense of dignity, a sense of divinity, a sense of awareness, and a sense of responsibility.

One hundred and fifty years ago, Napoleon set out to conquer the world. Like other conquerors before and since, his gross ambition led to failure. Among the armies that he sent in every direction was one that went to Egypt. One day in 1799 a certain Lieutenant

Boussard, attached to one of Napoleon's armies, was strolling near the village of Rosetta, located near the mouth of the Nile River. He happened to notice a stone protruding from the ground with three sets of inscriptions on it in three languages or types of writing. He called the attention of his superiors to this interesting item, and it was not long before scholars throughout the world were greatly intrigued. So important was the Rosetta stone that it was specifically mentioned in the treaty of peace, which provided that it should become the property of Great Britain. It eventually was placed in the British Museum.

The significance of the Rosetta stone, which was proved to have been written in 196 BC, was that the top portion was in Egyptian hieroglyphics, the classical writing of the times for monuments; the second section was in demotic writing, the everyday writing of the times; and the third was in Greek. It was surmised that the same message was written in three different ways, which later proved to be true, and thus from the Greek the translation of the demotic and hieroglyphic writing could be determined.

For forty years one scholar after another worked on it. A man named Champollion, who spent his whole career at it, finally decoded it. The message was insignificant but it was a great milestone in determining the history of our alphabet and of writing generally. From this discovery and many others like it over a period of many years has come a well-documented story of our alphabet and our language, through history. Oscar Ogg tells this fascinating story in his book, *The Twenty-six Letters*:

Think for a moment of our Christian era as existing for less than 2,000 years, of our whole Western Hemisphere having been discovered less than 500 years ago, and our own nation having existed for about 150 years. Against those periods of time, think, if you will, of these facts as presented by scientists: From the first flint weapon to the first cave drawing was a period of 230,000 years; from the time of cave drawings to hieroglyphics, another 15,000 years. From hieroglyphics to the Roman letters another 5,000 years, and from Roman letters to the invention of printing in 1454, 1,500 more years.

A sense of history gives one a perspective on current events. Modern waves or movements of one kind or another may seem extremely important in relation to our lifetime, but on the sea of time they are tiny ripples. A study of the history of scientific discovery, a study of the history of geographical discovery—all history, in fact, develops a sense of proportion, throws light upon current problems, and provides roots of stability against the squalls of the present. Surely a person of understanding must have a sense of history.

The second sense we are suggesting is a sense of dignity. That is, the dignity and individuality of each person. The miracle of all ages is the birth of a child. What a marvel is the study of heredity. How amazing is the fact that no two individuals are identical, even to their fingerprints. History may say that the great contribution of our age is the establishing of the individuality, the equality, and the dignity of woman; the importance of the individual. We may take great pride in the noble expression of the founders of our country when they said, "We hold these truths to be self evident, that all men are created equal; that they are endowed by their Creator with certain inalienable rights; that among these are life, liberty, and the pursuit of happiness." We do not argue the point; we do not offer proof. "We hold these truths to be *self-evident,* that all men are created equal." That they are endowed, *by their Creator,* with certain inalienable rights—life, liberty and the pursuit of happiness." This dignity of woman, this importance of the individual, is certainly a foundation of conception to the person of understanding. So we say, a woman of understanding needs a sense of dignity.

Now we come to the third, a sense of divinity. One evening, several weeks ago, a friend and I went to see a movie of Laurence Olivier's production of *Hamlet*, in Winnipeg. We were tremendously impressed, in fact, moved, by the excellence of this work. I shall never forget the portrayal of the scene where Laertes is about to leave home and Polonius is giving him advice which includes the great line, "This above all—to thine own self be true; and it must follow, as the night to day, thou canst not then be false to any man."

As we left the theater my friend asked, "How many people will be moved to attend church next Sunday because of having seen this movie tonight?" We explored the thought that any great art, great music, or any ennobling experience tends to quicken our sense of the divine. Life has little significance without the overtone of divinity. We may express our religious faiths in various ways, and our conceptions of God may vary, but any person of understanding who surveys the sweep of history, who senses the dignity of woman, will also have a sense of the divine.

The fourth sense that we suggested is a sense of awareness. It has been said, somewhat callously perhaps, that there are three kinds of people: those who make things happen, those who stand on the sidelines and watch, and those who don't know what is going on.

Probably no finer example can be found of an individual who exposed himself to life, who met it head on, who explored it with a keen sense of curiosity, than Benjamin Franklin. Do you remember the story of his first trip across the Atlantic Ocean? He provided himself with a large thermometer and each day of the voyage, at the same hour, he lowered the thermometer into the water and recorded the temperature. He was interested to note that each day, for the first few days, the temperature dropped, indicating colder water as they progressed into the ocean; but then for some reason the water began to warm up and there was a period of some days of warmer temperatures before the pattern again was reestablished of colder water as they reached the center of the ocean. Franklin reported this to a scientific society in London, which instituted a further study, which led to the discovery of the Gulf Stream. That was just one of the many significant contributions that Benjamin Franklin made through a sense of awareness, a sense of interest in his surroundings and the situations that he encountered.

The other day, on a Saturday morning at home, I received a call from a friend of mine who reported, in excited tones, "There's a flock of evening grosbeaks down in College Park." Lovers of birds know that evening grosbeaks are rare in this part of the country. My friend had never before seen one, and neither had I. We spread the word to a few other interested parties and soon a little group gathered down at College Park, and sure enough here was a flock of thirty to forty evening grosbeaks. One lady was so thrilled at seeing evening grosbeaks for the first time in her life, that not only was it a highlight of the day but will be one of the milestones of this year for her. The man who made the discovery was on his way to work, as thousands of others were that morning. He happened to notice birds that didn't fit into the pattern of his recognition. He stopped to investigate and made a discovery, which, while not earth-shaking, was certainly enriching to himself and to his friends.

A sense of history is important, a sense of the dignity and importance of woman is fundamental, and a sense of divinity is vital, but a person could have all of these and still exert no particular influence on others and leave no impact on society for having lived. When she adds to the other three a sense of awareness she begins to be in the position of making a contribution. But there is still one more, the sense of responsibility.

One of the most thrilling examples of a sense of responsibility is found in the parable of the Good Samaritan. You remember, a certain man was on the road to Jericho and fell among thieves. He was left by the side of the road to die. Several travellers passed by, aware of his presence and his condition, but with no sense of personal responsibility. The Good Samaritan took "the certain man" and saw to it that he was properly cared for.

In facing social problems, in solving political problems, in activities of our churches, in every organizational activity, we continually must fight against apathies and indifference. It is true that no people who have ever lived are subjected to such a barrage of information, reports, demands, from all over the world as are we—yet this has tended to develop callousness rather than sensitivity. A sense of responsibility, coupled with a sense of history, dignity, divinity and awareness, can work wonders. Think what Joan of Arc did for France, what Florence Nightingale did for nursing, what Emma Willard did for education, what hosts of other women, almost single handedly, have done for society and the world.

It is essential to a sense of responsibility to have a feeling of the close relationship and interweaving of all womankind. We cannot live to ourselves alone. We are interdependent one on another. No one has expressed this finer than the great English writer John Donne, who said:

No man is an island, entire of itself;
Every man is a piece of the Continent, a part of the main;
If a clod be washed away by the sea, Europe is the less,
As well as if a promontory were,
As well as if a manor of they friends
Or of thine own were.
Any man's death diminishes me,
because I am involved in Mankind;
And therefore never send to know
for whom the bell tolls;
It tolls for thee.

When woman is born she is endowed with the five physical senses. If she is to become a woman of understanding she must acquire, with effort, the five social senses.

—April 15, 1950

FAIR HOUSING FOR ALL

The idea that people should be allowed to live wherever they choose and can afford to live, regardless of their race, is so widely accepted in America today that it's hard to realize that just forty years ago, it was a controversial notion. In 1959, when the St. Paul City Council was considering an ordinance banning racial discrimination in housing practices, proponents of the idea had difficulty finding people in public life who were willing to go on record in its support. They couldn't get a single public office holder to come and speak at a City Council hearing. I was out of office, having just retired from the state Senate and not yet a candidate for governor. Nevertheless, they called me. I had carried the Fair Employment Practices Act in the state Senate when it was enacted in 1955, so they suspected that I would be sympathetic to the ordinance. They pleaded, "Won't you please come? We really need some help." I did not hesitate, even though I had to rearrange my schedule. I felt so strongly then, and feel as strongly now, that equal rights for everyone are imperative.

It was especially important in St. Paul in 1959 that people of color be assured of nondiscriminatory housing practices. An interstate highway, I-94, was about to be built through the heart of St. Paul's oldest and largest black section, the Rondo neighborhood. People there had to relocate. Already, some were encountering difficulty moving into other parts of the city. There was need for an ordinance to open the whole city to mixed racial residency. Unless that happened, another ghetto would form in a new location. Resistance to the ordinance was strong—but it did pass, and helped St. Paul become the city of diversity and opportunity for all that it is today.

Here, in its entirety, is what I said to the City Council:

⏭ When I was asked to appear at this hearing, I put aside other things and came. All of us should do all we can to make progress in improving human relationships among all our citizens. There are but a few observations I would make.

Our city and its people are to be commended for the progress that has been made in eliminating discrimination. I know that our mayor and each member of this council would yield to no one in affirming the right of every person to have the full benefits of American citizenship and opportunity. We can also agree that we are here dealing with a sensitive subject fraught with misunderstanding that will require the wisdom and courage of this council.

We must eliminate housing discrimination simply because all discrimination based on race, color, or creed must be abolished from our land. We must eliminate housing discrimination in St. Paul now, because of the practical problem arising from the freeway construction. All sections of our city should be prepared to accept new neighbors on their merit as individuals without regard to race, color, or creed.

I would ask those who feel injury might come to them if this ordinance is passed to weigh that possible injury against the unhappiness, humiliation and frustration of others. Is it Christian, or in accord with the principles of any faith, that we should think in terms of our own security and comfort without showing at least equal concern for the security and comfort of all who share this country with us? If we are willing to force a man to sell his home to build a highway, we should not balk at prohibiting voluntary sales in a manner hurtful to our society.

I cannot refer to the specific language of the ordinance before you but I would hope it would declare an end to discrimination in all housing transactions, set up a commission to carry on an educational and operating program, and include enforcement provisions. Those who work to these ends will be remembered as builders of the true America. Those who oppose them are vestiges of a fading past.

—May 22, 1959

CHILDREN & POVERTY

Most, if not all, Americans would agree that raising children in poverty, without adequate nutrition, shelter or health care, damages not only those children, but also the whole nation. Yet this nation of vast resources has not yet found a way to assure every American child a start in life that is free of the scourge of poverty.

In 1969, I spoke about an idea for more directly and forcefully addressing the problem of childhood poverty. I would change little in my recommendation today. I still believe we need a comprehensive national program to assure that no child goes without life's basic necessities. There needs to be recognition that those who have children make a contribution to the whole society, and deserve the whole society's support.

Americans can see through the example of just one area —health care—that a system of privatized social services in which the government helps only a few is inadequate and inequitable. Too many people, children and adults, are left out completely. Children particularly suffer when there is a shortage of adequate medical care.

One area of particular concern to me as an employer has been the need for working parents to have adequate time to nurture their children. The latest research all points to the importance to a child's brain development of having an intimate, intense relationship with one or two adults in the first three years of life. Allowing time for that bonding is why at ECM Publishing, we established a parenting leave program that has been recognized as one of the most generous in Minnesota. We allow parents of children under age three, mothers and fathers alike, up to a full year's leave of absence at 40 percent pay. An employee is eligible to take up to three parenting leaves during his or her career at ECM.

Our parenting leave policy is an investment in this nation's future—one I am pleased to make. But I hope that an enlightened government will own up to its responsibility in this regard. The state ought to provide a new parent a stipend of one third of his or her regular pay, which the employer would match, so that the employee would get two thirds of his or her regular pay during parenting leave. Further, I think a leave of up to three years should be allowed. That might seem like a great interference with a career. But I liken it to soldiers going to war, and being promised their old jobs back with no restriction on how long they may be gone. The same kind of thinking should be applied to raising children.

Americans have clung for too long to the unfortunate idea that parents who receive cash support for caring for their children are undeserving. This speech sets forth a mechanism that might make payment of cash benefits to parents more acceptable, in the same way that Social Security payments are. Such payments should be understood as earned, through the work of parenting, so that people can accept it with self-respect, not as a dole.

Here is some of what I said in May, 1969, to the National Conference on Social Welfare in New York City:

⏭ State and local government cannot be seen today as coping satisfactorily with the enormous welfare problems that command attention. I cannot bring myself to concentrate on the role of state and local government only. I believe we are in a national crisis—a crisis of need, a crisis of finances and a crisis of public attitude. We need sweeping changes, on the basis of a massive national effort.

A landmark decision of the U. S. Supreme Court may be the key to the substantial changes in approach so clearly needed. As you well know, our Supreme Court has abolished residence requirements of the states to qualify for public assistance. Everyone agrees that an instant result of the finding will be an overwhelming demand for minimum national standards. Otherwise, we can expect huge migration from low standard states to higher, and from no-program rural areas to cities.

The suggestion of national standards and national funding has had support apart from the Supreme Court decision. The Advisory Commission on Inter-governmental Relations urged that the federal government pay all welfare costs, and that the states finance most of the cost of schooling. The panel said the federal government had "superior fiscal capacity" to deal with the increasing mobility of poor people. Obviously, if the federal government were to pay all welfare costs, the federal government would have to establish national minimum standards.

In a recent talk in Minneapolis, Alvin Schorr [a leading administrator of the federal War on Poverty] made an interesting point in reference to psychological reactions to various forms of subsidies and grants. Welfare payments in almost all forms have come under severe attack. People seem to want to discredit the payments as justification for their reduction or elimination. There is one exception Mr. Schorr noted—the Social Security program of payments to older citizens. This is a socially acceptable payment. There is no great outcry about misuse of funds received by any of the beneficiaries. It is paid and received in an atmosphere of dignity that attends no comparable program. Why? For two main reasons: One, nearly everyone is eligible to receive it. It is universal. Secondly, it has been presented as an insurance program, so people feel entitled to receive what they have been paying for.

Actually, of course, half of the contributions are payments made as a tax on the employer's payroll. Furthermore, in a very great many cases, there is little relationship between the amounts received in benefits and the amounts paid in. It is surely far from a fully funded insurance program. It is heavily weighted in favor of lower income people, and thus becomes a tax-supported subsidy to older people to a far greater degree than it is a true insurance program. However, it has gained the aura of respectability through universality, some personal contribution, and acceptance of the title "insurance."

Rather than criticizing, we must borrow these features of Social Security and introduce them into other welfare programs. With this in mind, I would endorse New York Governor Nelson Rockefeller's suggestion of a national compulsory health insurance program, financed by employer-employee contributions, to take the pressure off rising Medicaid costs, which are financed by the federal, state and local governments. It is also my belief that the plan of children's allowances should be made a part of a new national social services program. The payments could be $50 per-month for children under six and $10 per month for those ages six to eighteen. This should be a universal payment to all families, and could be made in lieu of the present income tax deduction per dependent.

Children's allowances would be an excellent form of income maintenance, made more acceptable if made universal and if financed by employer-employee funding. It has the advantage of aiding all families at a time when extra income can be most helpful, and would be particularly beneficial to parents of pre-school children. It would not offend my sensibilities if the employer-employee funding was insufficient to pay the total cost of the program and that other forms of taxation were used. These elements are mentioned not as a total program, but key parts of a total program of sufficient dimension, and on a national basis.

I believe that in matters relating to the basic needs of our people, we can no longer function as fifty individual states, but must unite and act as one nation. Not only must we eliminate barriers of residence requirements, but also every other restriction that inhibits meeting the essential needs of every family in our country. This is not a question of government doing something for undeserving people, but rather a matter of a decent society of concerned people using governmental mechanics to put a minimum support floor under all families. If this is denied, the greatest damage is done to innocent children, and problems accumulate for future generations to face.

I believe the greatest service state and local officials, boards of private agencies, and everyone else in any way connected with the social service programs of our country can render is to impress on President Nixon and members of the Congress in the most vigorous way possible that a nationally funded and broadly expanded social service program is the most urgent national problem we have. It is an emergency that compels greater priority than the Vietnam War, the ABM missile system, and the space program, all of which are laying heavy claims on our national resources. Somehow the means must be found to stir our people so the political leaders will respond with programs of the dimensions and imagination that the times require. This is where the leverage of the states must be placed right now.

Some suggestions have been made of solving problems by greater use of private enterprise. Certainly this should be explored, and is worth some trial. One limitation is that industry is not schooled in patience with inadequate or difficult people. Industry has had great freedom to hire and fire with little regard to social consequences. It will require some re-orientation for private enterprise to work with people who have been the victims of deprivation, discrimination, and sub-standard education, health, and social opportunities. They cannot be hired and fired. They must be patiently worked with for years if we are to break the cycle that has brought such a disastrous situation as now exists in the poverty belt that permeates so much of our land.

Nevertheless, the private enterprise approach is worth a trial for, if nothing else, it may be the best way to acquaint an important segment of our society with the intense difficulty of solving some of these tough human problems, and the pressing need for a major national effort.

We must recognize that we have a national emergency of major proportions on our hands. It must be given priority over other matters now commanding our resources. The alternatives should be put squarely before the people. If the American people had a choice right now to end our commitment in Vietnam, and forget about the ABM missile system, and put the funds employed there into essential domestic programs, there is no question in my mind how they would vote.

—May 27, 1969

PUBLIC WELFARE: THE MYTH & THE REALITY

Americans are generally warm-hearted and generous when an isolated incidence of great need comes to their attention. There will be a voluntary outpouring of gifts, flowers and money, showing that the heart of our people is rich in concern for others. But when the effort to care for people who are unable to care for themselves is made by government, and is called relief or public welfare, a dichotomy is evident. People tend to believe that there is abuse, that the abuse is widespread, and that many people are receiving assistance because of laziness or character deficiencies, and ought not be supported.

Those beliefs are not grounded in fact. Research has shown that while there is always some abuse in welfare programs, it is no more than is found in almost any sphere of human activity. The cheaters are a very small minority. My experience is that few people enjoy being on welfare. The most common attitude of welfare recipients is one of earnestness in wanting to be a self-supporting, proud citizen. Punitive approaches to such people are neither warranted nor worthy of the American people.

Welfare programs should be designed to help people help themselves. Many welfare recipients want to work, but cannot afford to, because of health care or child care needs. Minnesota has been a forerunner among the states with a program that keeps in touch with recipients after they are employed, and supplements their earnings with health and child care support to see them through the early stages of employment, until they can be fully self-sufficient. That's a wise approach to public welfare that is in keeping with its fundamental purpose.

Too many people think of welfare recipients as a class apart from the rest of the citizenry. In fact, in Minnesota, about one in ten people at any given time receive some government help with health care, child care, long-term care or income support that might be called "welfare" in the broad sense of the term. Moreover, a large share of Minnesota families will need that kind of help for some family member at some point in their lives. Welfare programs provide a backstop against many of life's setbacks, of the sort anyone might experience. If that fact were more widely recognized, the stigma attached to welfare might be lessened.

It was clear forty years ago that public support for welfare was waning, and that it behooved those of us who understand welfare's importance to come to its defense. That is what I tried to do in a number of speeches. Here are excerpts from two such addresses in the 1960s. The first, made while I was governor, addressed a regional conference of the Child Welfare League of America, meeting in Detroit.

⏭ Public welfare programs today are receiving closer public scrutiny than ever before. No one can ignore the fact that many of our fellow countrymen have not really accepted welfare as a program deserving the support of tax funds. The rejection of any individual or group of individuals who are not self-supporting or self-sufficient takes form in devious attempts to discredit those who are the beneficiaries of public help. Aid to Dependent Children is most frequently the subject of these attacks because moral considerations can so easily be introduced in connection with it. It also gives a not-so-subtle opportunity to express discriminatory attitudes toward minority groups.

We should not lull ourselves into righteous complacency by merely discrediting the motives of our attackers. Many of us were already worried about the effectiveness of our programs and uncomfortably aware of fragmented services, unmet needs, and of other weaknesses in welfare administration and community planning to better help people. We were eager to mobilize our services to remove the causes of dependency wherever possible, and to speed rehabilitation and restoration wherever this is possible, so as to minimize chronic dependency.

Minnesota had been trying to formulate a better way for organizing and extending social services. I am sure you have come upon references to the St. Paul "family centered project," now in its tenth year. Out of it has come a concept that we have adopted in our state welfare department which we call "work reorientation." [This was a precursor of today's Minnesota Family Investment Program.] The essential purpose is not complicated: to try to solve the problems presented by the families in our public welfare caseloads through rehabilitation in the cases where there is potentiality for it, and prevention of new problems where the danger signals can be detected. Not many people are likely to quarrel with these objectives. But has our past public welfare administration been systematically organized around these deliberate operational goals? I don't think we can say that it has.

Here's where the "reorienting" comes in. It means adopting new methods in our daily welfare work. It means systematically analyzing the total family and its problems, rather than concentrating on the eligibility of one or more family members for assistance. It means making organized judgments about the potential for change in each case. It means reorganizing our staffing patterns, so that we concentrate on those cases where sustained effort is required to meet rehabilitative goals. It means developing one organized family plan, enlisting the aid of other community welfare resources as required to see it through. It means regular evaluation, so that we can accurately report to our communities about what kinds of problems we face, what the outlook is, and how we are coming along. The answer to welfare's critics is not to cast people on a slag pile of humanity, but to accept the challenge of each human problem, and work away at it.

—March 29, 1962

These remarks come from a 1968 address to a regional conference of the American Public Welfare Association, in St. Paul.

⏭ In all the attack on welfare there obviously is implied criticism of those who have been administering and working in these programs.

In my experience with social workers and administrators of social work programs, I have met great people who are for the most part completely dedicated, highly trained and most competent. They work with too little help in attempting an almost insurmountable task on skimpy budgets, and are suffocated by the numbers of people seeking or needing their service. I salute the social work profession and I truly admire it greatly. Yet we must recognize that it is in a crisis of failure. Why?

The professionalism of social work in the past twenty-five years has brought great benefits but it has also brought some problems that have grown to dimensions that need attention. One is in the field of communication. Social work jargon has become frightening to legislators and unintelligible to many others. Social workers ought to speak in plain English that anyone can understand. Also, with professionalism comes an unemotional objectivity that is not conducive to stirring people's emotions, and they need to be stirred. I believe we must have crusading zealots who will fight for the rights of the silent suffering thousands upon thousands of children, for example, without the basic necessities of a loving family, sufficient food, shelter, medical care and all the rest. Who knows this need better than you—and if you can play it cool, how can others be expected to be stirred to energetic concern?

The present general impression is that we are spending a vast amount of money on welfare, that we get relatively little for it, and that the program is loaded with abuse. The fact is that relative to our affluence, relative to the need, and relative to the percent of gross national product other much smaller and poorer nations spend, we have spent nowhere near enough. We have relegated child welfare in our country to a low priority when it deserves the highest.

The other fact from survey after survey is that although abuse does exist and should be rooted out, it occurs in but a small percentage of the cases. In law we have a long tradition of preferring many guilty accused to go free rather than suffer one innocent to be condemned in error. In welfare, we seem bent upon denying necessary services to thousands of children if that be necessary to render a moral judgment on a few offending mothers, even though, in the process, the children suffer far more than the mothers.

Some people recoil from the shock of our shortcomings [in providing life's necessities for poor children] with the belief that even though we fall short, our nation does better by its people than do others. We can justifiably boast of the highest level of scientific medicine in the world, but we lag behind a dozen countries in our provisions for prenatal and post-natal care, for example. The children of the poor tend to disappear from sight once they are born, and are rarely seen by a physician except in cases of the most extreme gravity. One study recently concluded that one of the main dangers to the nation's children is the fantastic network of eligibility requirements and restrictive limitations that, in the name of accountability, enmeshes public welfare in the United States.

There must be a realization that what is required is a multiplication of our effort, quite the contrary to thinking of welfare as one of the domestic programs that must give way to the requirements of military spending. I believe the reality is crisis, but not defeat. I believe the challenge is reappraisal and a new realization that in your determined public leadership lies the hope of millions of our people. Your greater task may be with the citizenry than with your clients.

—April 28, 1968

NATIVE AMERICANS

The native American population of Minnesota has always been a source of fascination for me. I had a rare opportunity to pursue that interest as governor. During the summer of 1962, I toured every reservation in the state, met with tribal leaders, and learned a great deal about their proud heritage and present-day problems. I was proud to be taken in as a member of the White Earth Reservation band of Ojibwe, and to have a particularly close association with them.

Not long after that tour, I addressed the Fourth Annual Retreat for the Lutheran Church and the American Indian at Augsburg College. I was full of strong impressions and feelings about what I had seen and learned. One thing that bothered me very much was the difficulty Indian children had when they were forced to leave the reservations and go into towns for school, beginning with the seventh grade. They didn't have clothes. They didn't even have soap. They couldn't compete with the children in school. They were ostracized for conditions far beyond their control, so they didn't get through high school. It was a shame, because one of the great needs these young people had was for education.

In the intervening years, prosperity finally has come to some of Minnesota's tribes, because of their monopoly control of casino gambling in the state. But the wealth has not been uniformly distributed. Many native people have not shared in the gambling bonanza. Still, where there has been good tribal leadership, casino profits have resulted in improved streets, new health clinics, better schools, better water quality, and a better way of life generally.

Despite those benefits of modern life, there are signs that some Indians want to roll back history. There's a situation now in Mille Lacs County, in which the Indian community of Mille Lacs wants to recreate the original reservation boundaries, which have long since been eroded. That would be a mistake. I think Indians need to accept life as it is today and adjust to today's living, instead of trying to undo the wrongs of the past or reestablish things that have long since changed. I'd like to see them look toward a plan of integration. I don't think two nations with separate laws can live together successfully. I think that, somehow, we have to work out a fair, equitable, kind arrangement of integration, rather than continue to have nations living within a nation. Within the next hundred years, I think a goal should be integration of the Indian nations with the rest of the people of the United States.

Here is what I said about Indian-white relations in 1962:

⏭ Understanding on the part of the individual is the key to eliminating racial discrimination. The more you understand about a person, the clearer becomes his place in the scheme of things. Understanding on the part of every individual is fundamental to solving the problems American Indians face. We must understand that all people have differences and learn to accept others as individuals, on their individual merit. Indians share a heritage different than ours; many of their customs and beliefs are unlike ours. It is the blending of the contributions of the many societies that has made our country great.

Despite our state's fair employment laws, the Indian still has a real problem finding work. There seems to be a widespread, but very erroneous, belief that Indians are not good workers. One of the responsibilities of understanding is to realize that Indians can be just as responsible and just as hard-working as any other group.

This month the National Association of County Attorneys named the outstanding county attorney in the United States. This is the first time that any person has been so honored by the association. Edward Rogers, the nation's outstanding county attorney for 1962, happens to be the county attorney in Cass County, Minnesota. He is eighty-six years old and has been county attorney for thirty-six years. Ed Rogers has achieved great success in his career and is a very respected individual, not only in his community, but in the nation as well. This is a marvelous achievement for any person, but I think that it is a particularly marvelous achievement for Ed Rogers, because he is an Indian. This man worked hard and overcame the discrimination that faces his people.

Some Indian families and individuals will get along very well, use every opportunity to make their way and establish themselves as fine, respectable citizens. Others will make a mess of their lives no matter how much effort is put forth to help and guide them. We must realize that this is a characteristic of white people, Negroes and all other people as well.

The Indians I know are among the most sensitive people that I have ever met. They are kind, generous, and friendly. I have noticed that there is a great drive among some Indians to work, build, grow and get ahead. In many cases I have observed, if a family does well and gets ahead, it becomes a magnet for the rest of the relatives. Things go well for one family and soon there are three families. Indians have a natural desire to share. They are so kind and generous to each other that it is difficult for a family to become what we would consider independent.

Unemployment among Indians is a problem that can only be solved by a great deal more individual understanding of Indian culture by the larger society. As I have met and become acquainted with my many Indian friends, I realized that one of the things they retain is a love of freedom, which is not always compatible with our slavishness to time clocks and daily routine. Steady employment can be an enormous adjustment for an Indian. Yet it is fundamental to the financial stability of a family.

One thing that I feel will be of considerable help is the recently opened American Indian Employment and Guidance Center, established to specifically aid Indians in obtaining employment. The discrimination toward those who are seeking employment or have been laid off was one of the reasons for the opening of the employment center.

Programs to aid Indian people should have as their fundamental philosophy to help the Indian help himself. I feel that it is very important to lift the sights of the young Indians and restore their pride in the great tradition and heritage of the American Indian. I will always remember the moment I was made a member of the White Earth Band of the Chippewa tribe by one of the noblest men I have ever met—George Selkirk, chief of the White Earth Band. Chief Little White Cloud (George Selkirk) is a truly great individual. I will never forget when he stood up during the ceremony, elderly but straight, noble of voice—I'll tell you, he is proud of his Chippewa heritage. This is what we must encourage in Indian youth.

We have initiated a pilot project, the Minnesota Indian Guides, to help achieve this end. We picked about a dozen fine boys from the Red Lake Indian Reservation, assigned two counselors to work with them and gave them a short training course. They are to serve as guides to tourists who would like to tour the Red Lake Indian Reservation. They show them the lumbering and fishing operations and relate the history of the Chippewa of Minnesota. This program is providing employment, but even more important, it is providing training, and acting as a psychological stimulant. I hope that this program will inspire these young fellows and restore their pride. They are Indian Guides, representatives of their people. They will grow in stature and vision. I would like to see this program grow and spread to all parts of our state, so that to be an Indian Guide will be a symbol of achievement.

We must learn to accept people as individuals, and accept individual differences as a matter of course. I think that we are making progress, but we should not be satisfied with gradual progress. The time has come to eliminate discrimination and to work intensively to secure freedom and opportunity for every single person.

—August 1, 1962

INDUSTRY'S ROLE IN SOCIAL SERVICE

In 1968, leaders in industry were coming to realize the importance for our whole society of employing members of racial minorities. At H. B. Fuller Company, we wanted to do our share, so we hired some black workers who had formerly been welfare recipients. A difficulty was immediately apparent. Our new employees were not accustomed to the discipline of a workday. They would come late, leave early, and be absent rather casually. The other workers in the plant criticized them mercilessly and almost drove them out of the place. I had the idea that social workers were needed on site to help the new employees and ease them over the transition to a life of discipline. I still think it's a good idea.

There has been a great effort made in this country to remove people from welfare rolls and train them for employment. The plan was that welfare aid would stop after five years. People were told they had five years to shape up and get ready to be on their own. The message had a punitive air to it that I think dooms it to failure. Many human beings do not respond positively to punishment. As the five years is ending for the first wave of people to experience the cutoff rule, many are still unprepared for self-sufficiency.

Social service is needed for people who have become so alienated from the mainstream that they cannot conceive of relying on their own enterprise to support themselves. Such people need assistance in changing their attitudes—assistance that comes not from a degree of punishment, but from care for every human being, to make up for whatever deprivation has caused their condition. It's a difficult job in many cases, but industry could do it. Industry can do almost anything it undertakes. It performs miracles almost every day.

This country is only beginning to realize the high cost of not attempting to reach out to alienated people and make them productive citizens. The nation's prisons are overflowing, even in Minnesota, where we have historically had one of the lowest incarceration rates in the country. In some states, people are being released from prison before their terms are up simply because it's so costly to incarcerate them. That fact alone should make us aware that we need to have a constructive approach to human development and training, one tailored to the particular needs of every person. It's a very large task, but I believe it is the only way for Americans to be assured of peace and stability in our country.

Here's what I said about social work in the workplace in 1968 in Minneapolis, to the regional meeting of the National Association of Social Workers:

⏭ Recently I attended a breakfast meeting of Twin City businessmen called together to pledge jobs to the under-privileged unemployed in the ghettos of our Twin Cities. It was well attended, and reflected a sincere desire of those attending to help eliminate the cause of central city problems. Nevertheless, some of the comments gave me an uneasy feeling. "I'm willing to open up some jobs if they'll send me some people who are willing to work and will really appreciate a job," said one. "I tried to help last year," said another, "but the fellows who came didn't last a week." It was all too clear: Jobs alone will not solve the problems of unpreparedness, alienation, unrest, defiance and bitterness one finds prevalent today.

A week after the breakfast just described, I had a tour of the new St. Paul Area Vocational School. It is a wonderful facility, excellently staffed and equipped. It offers many courses in some thirty-nine fields, all practical, job-oriented programs. The school prides itself on its fine job placement record and the success of its graduates. One cannot help but be greatly impressed. However, it suddenly dawned on me as we walked from room to room that I had seen very few Negroes. The school is located on the edge of a heavily Negro residential area. I stopped, and turning to the principal, I said, "I'm suddenly surprised at how few Negroes I see, particularly in a vocational school offering training young Negroes so badly need, and on the edge of this heavily Negro area. Where are they?"

The principal said, "You touch a sensitive point with us. The fact is that we are running a practical program here. We cannot straighten out problem kids. In order to benefit from our program there must be strong motivation and hard work, and the sad fact is that most Negroes don't come with the attitudes we consider essential."

I left wondering where in the world we can begin to unravel the snarl of human relationships that plagues us. As I drove slowly back to my office, I began to wonder what chance a new concept of employment could have, a new responsibility for commerce and industry that today only a very few firms accept.

From the earliest days of the Industrial Revolution, there has been general acceptance of a hire-and-fire technique that sorted the satisfactory from the unsatisfactory employee. Likewise, people did not tend to criticize the firm that laid off large numbers of people when technological change rendered their work unneeded. Little concern was given to Negroes who always had the menial jobs and whose families drifted downward.

Larger and larger numbers of our citizens were being driven to poverty and degradation with little hope for betterment. Churches and private organizations endeavored to help, but to a greater and greater degree, direct relief from county government, old age assistance, aid to families with dependent children, Social Security and a host of other tax-supported programs carried the main load. Business complained about the welfare state and held appropriations as low as possible, never facing up to the fact that the discards and misfits, the deprived and discriminated against in commerce and industry, were much of the welfare burden. Most businessmen did not identify sympathetically with the problem or acknowledge their own responsibility. Furthermore, they were distinctly uncomfortable with social workers.

Valiantly as the social work profession has worked to emphasize rehabilitation, the suffocation of numbers has reduced many a caseworker, particularly in larger cities, to a tired eligibility-checker. The gap between the youngster in the deprived ghetto family and the requirements for admission to mainstream employment became very wide indeed. It's more than the social worker or teacher can manage, particularly when employment examinations and demanding personnel officers stand astride the path.

Public education never really started to move in our country until commerce and industry recognized that educated young people were essential to manning the offices and plants of a burgeoning economy. When all elements of our society got behind free public education, great strides were made. It is high time that every element of commerce and industry recognize that unless it truly and completely joins hands with public and private agencies, churches and schools in erasing poverty, eliminating prejudice, providing genuine opportunity for dignity and decency, the very system that provides private free enterprise will simply not survive, nor in the minds of increasing numbers, should it. The act of offering jobs and condemning those who do not measure up to established standards of conduct, motivation and effort is of little help.

Our chambers of commerce have convention bureaus that work with groups to bring their conventions to town, they have industrial development programs, legislative bureaus and many more useful agencies. To these, I would suggest adding a Department of Social Service to work closely with private and public social agencies, to bridge this employment gap. Just as cleverly devised campaigns at local and state levels tell the story of tourist attractions and industrial plant advantages, so I believe there must be a massive campaign beamed at the under-motivated, the bitter, the alienated, to change their attitudes, elevate their value judgments, point the way for genuine acceptance and achievement, and win them back to the mainstream of American life.

I believe that individual plants should have directors of social service—people with social-work training and casework experience who will do family casework with recruited workers from ghetto areas, and also direct in-depth psychological work with the work force to eliminate prejudice and bigotry and provide a comfortable environment for all employees. Another function will be to aid workers and families over the hurdles of serious problems—alcoholism, mental illness, family discord—rather than passing the problem along by discharging offending individuals.

Instead of social work being segregated in government and private agencies, where it has tended to become institutionalized and alienated, I am suggesting that commerce and industry, realizing the serious challenge to its own existence, move large segments of social work right into the plant, into the chambers of commerce, into the unions, into the offices of trade. It strikes me this would offer a chance for bringing problems and solutions closer together and establish a more direct line from the degradation of poverty to the dignity of self-support.

Fortunately we see some evidences of business concern through such organizations as the Urban Coalition, but much of this has been limited to lining up jobs, which, as we have pointed out, is a vastly over-simplified approach. Government alone, industry alone, and surely the deprived alone cannot work out of our predicament. There must be a joining of forces and recognition of a new concept of social responsibility by industry and the acceptance of the special competence of social workers as an important element in the success of economic enterprise.

I recently heard a fantastic talk on the true dimension of our space achievements. Within fifteen months we'll have a man on the moon. I do not decry these achievements, for they prove to me that our problem is not one of ability to do for our society a job of the same dimensions we are doing in space, but the simpler one of determining our objectives. I challenge business and industry to invite social work into the establishment, to generate the necessary investments, to create the essential attitudes that will resolve the frustration and eliminate the bitter differences now tearing down the fiber of our society.

—May 22, 1968

OUR AGING CITIZENS

Meeting the needs of frail, elderly people was an issue for Minnesota when I was governor. It saddens me to realize that, forty years later, this state is still struggling with how best to provide and pay for the care needed by aged people in failing health. In the 1960s, Congress enacted Medicare, and there was hope that the nation would make the well-being of elderly Americans a national responsibility. It's regrettable that Medicare failed to cover the fast-growing costs of long-term care and prescription drugs. A question that deserves more debate today is whether the United States should provide universal health care under federal auspices, with a single-payer plan.

For Eleanor and me, these are personal concerns as well as policy questions. We have been able to obtain care in our own home, but many of our friends and relatives have not been so fortunate. We have seen how strained the long-term care system is, how costly medicines are, how overworked and underpaid are care providers. Around-the-clock health care is expensive but unavoidably necessary for many people. Minnesota cannot fail to meet that need and still claim to be a humane state.

Minnesota was the first state to provide nursing home care at public expense. But nursing home care doesn't meet all the needs of older people, particularly their needs for independence, productive activity and involvement with the larger society. Older people with physical handicaps can live useful lives if they're given some help. Eleanor and I are seeing that, even at ninety-two and ninety-four, we can keep relatively active. Having good health care makes all the difference.

Here is what I said to the 1963 legislature on this topic:

⏭ One of Minnesota's prime concerns is for a priceless human resource, its growing number of senior citizens, age 65 and over. They represent no less than 10.4 per cent of our population, and as a result Minnesota ranks eleventh across the nation in numbers of senior citizens. Just as the population of older people is growing in Minnesota, so the average life-span is stretching. In 1900 the average Minnesotan lived only 48 years, an age which is virtually on the threshold of achievement for many of us today. In 1962 the span extended to 72. No longer is the two-generation family over 65 rare. Happily, an eightieth birthday is no longer unusual, and the newspapers of our state record that the 100-year age mark is being attained with some regularity in community after community.

The growing number of older citizens provides two-fold testimony that Minnesota's future is bright. First, longer-living Minnesotans testify to our invigorating climate, superb recreational advantages and excellent medical care, and serve as living inducements to others to come to this state to work and build their futures. Second, our older people serve as great moral and intellectual ballast, providing matchless experience, stability, maturity and wisdom gleaned from useful living. It would be tragic if this great resource were not more fully utilized. The task of building a better Minnesota cannot be conceded solely to the young. We need the benefit of those who have gone before to shape the new dimensions of the future.

Minnesota has benefited from a sound program for the aging. The state program is based on two principles: that problems should be solved on the local community level, and that the older citizen should be allowed to live as independently as possible. These are wise guidelines. Within this framework, much has been done to meet our responsibility to those who are older. The responsibility has been met with savings to the state, and resultant benefits to our people.

I am thinking particularly of one county where an ailing elderly couple faced the possibility of entering a nursing home at state expense, but who were provided more individual attention and personal care in their home by means of a homemaker program undertaken with the county public health nursing service. The result: In human terms, which are always the first concern, the couple received dutiful care in the familiar surroundings of their own home. In economic terms, consideration of which in these days of rising costs is also a factor, a net saving of $2,400 per individual was effected.

Since the legislature created the Governor's Citizens Council on Aging, much has been accomplished within the framework of individual independence and state-local action. There are thirty-three local or county committees on aging. Operation of day centers, planning of leisure-time activities, organization of "Golden Age Clubs" and surveys of community resources, including housing needs, constitute a well-balanced program for older citizens. The value of this program can be best seen on a local scale. The Aitkin County Committee on Aging has pointed out that since the opening of their day center, there have been no commitments of elderly persons to state institutions.

Minnesota must move ahead to further implement this program. I recommend the following:

1. **Housing:** There is a significant lack of appropriate housing for the older citizen, particularly in the low-income group. While urban areas have taken great steps to provide for public housing, the rural counties represent the highest incidence of older citizens (about 17 percent). The power to establish public housing within Minnesota is limited to cities, villages and boroughs. Therefore no county can provide public housing to meet the needs of its low-income older citizens, many of whom have most inadequate housing. Therefore I recommend remedial legislation to include counties in the definition of the Municipal and Housing Redevelopment Act, to enable counties to assist local communities in meeting the housing needs of their low income elderly.

2. **Medical care for the aged:** Minnesotans can be proud of the fact that our state program of Old Age Assistance allows senior citizens to receive full medical care as it is required. The fact that many first applications for Old Age Assistance stem from a medical emergency or prolonged illness leads to the conclusion that the Medical Assistance Act [federal legislation that was a forerunner of Medicare] could cover the cost of such emergencies and illnesses, allowing older citizens to remain otherwise independent. As this legislation could provide for some 30 per cent of our older citizens, I urge the legislature to adopt legislation to implement this program in Minnesota.

3. **Old Age Assistance**: To comply with the new federal regulation, legislative action is required which would exempt up to $30 per month of earned income in determining the grant of an old age assistance recipient.

4. **Tax relief:** Tax relief for the older citizen is a recurring concern. The Housing Committee of the Governor's Citizens Council on Aging has recommended that modification of the laws for the 65-year-old homeowner was advisable and recommended that the age 65 and older homeowner could receive, upon application, help in paying one-half of his homestead tax assessment, not to exceed $200 in any one year. I wholeheartedly endorse and urge you to consider this proposal.

—March 4, 1963

ALCOHOLISM

H. B. Fuller employed several people who had drinking problems and gradually became alcoholics. Before treatment was available for such addictions, employers generally handled such cases with a pink slip. Sadly, at Fuller, we finally released one talented fellow, after we had struggled with his illness for many years and felt we had no other recourse. He had supervision over others, and we ultimately couldn't stand for him inflicting his conduct on them. I hated to let him go, because I liked him very much. I had traveled with him as a salesman. But the minute he was on his own, he would get into a compulsive drinking situation. Sadly, he died an alcoholic.

When I entered the legislature in 1949, that man was on my mind. I wanted to see what the state was doing about alcohol problems among its workforce. I found that the state considered alcoholism a social problem, not a disease. The rule was to fire alcoholic employees who did not perform well. I helped set up an interim study commission that laid the groundwork for a state policy establishing alcoholism as a health problem, and launched the first state alcoholism recovery program.

Addiction remains a very serious problem in our society, with other drugs joining alcohol as the addictive substances of choice. Drugs are so debilitating that one hesitates to advocate their legalization. But one advantage of a long life is that I can recall things that others must study as history. I remember Prohibition. It fostered illicit dealing in liquor, and led to the growth of organized crime. That hurt American society. Society is being hurt today by much the same policy approach to addictive drugs. What's more, our drug laws result in a lot of people going to jail for the possession of rather small amounts of illegal substances. These laws are filling up our jails with minor offenders. Criminal conduct is better defined as someone taking advantage of someone else. When people are injuring themselves only, a little different approach ought to be possible. In a limited way, and with careful controls, some legalization of milder drugs might be in order.

As a legislator and as governor, I tried to draw attention to the problem of alcohol addiction and to praise the work of Alcoholics Anonymous, an organization I much admire. I spoke with several Alcoholics Anonymous chapters. Here's some of what I said at one such occasion:

⏭ There is probably no other disease so completely devastating to the mind, spirit and body of a man as alcoholism. The work of Alcoholics Anonymous offers the hope of conquering this affliction, and the courage to face the continuing challenges this personal battle presents.

The United States Department of Health considers alcoholism the fourth most important public health problem in the United States. Alcoholism is not confined to any particular segment of our population. It strikes rich and poor, professional people and labor forces, men and women. A national survey by the Ethyl Corporation found that three out of every 100 persons in industry were alcoholics. In fact, alcoholism in industry is one of our most serious problems today. No occupational or social group is immune to alcoholism.

Many years ago I knew an individual who had once been a very successful salesman for Tennessee Coal and Iron. His job as a salesman required that he do considerable traveling, and he frequently was away from home for long periods. While spending lonely nights in hotels, he got into the habit of drinking. Eventually he lost control and became an alcoholic. As a result, he couldn't perform his work and he lost his job and many of his friends, and caused his family considerable hardship.

Finally, he came to grips with himself, realized his condition and joined the local Alcoholics Anonymous chapter. Well, this fellow "dried out" and stayed dry, but not without terrific struggles to keep away from alcohol during the first few months of his membership in AA. He fought down his temptations and regained control of his life, and restored his self-respect. A few years later he joined the faculty of the University of Wisconsin as a professor of business administration. Before he retired, he was recognized as one of the best professors in the College of Business Administration, and was one of the professors best liked by the students.

This man overcame his problem, but not without hard work, determination and an abiding faith in God. He once again became a well-liked and prominent member of society. You have taken that first and most important step—that of recognizing the problem exists—and you have sought help in solving it. May your every effort be crowned with success, and the years before you filled with the good things of life.

—May 24, 1962

III. BUSINESS

BEYOND THE BOTTOM LINE : WHAT BUSINESS ADDS TO COMMUNITY LIFE

People often tend to underrate the public service dimension of business. There can be noble motives behind a business. Providing employment for people is important. Supplying new and better products is important. If those things are put first, and making money behind them in priority, and then concern for the environment and the community in which the business exists added behind those three aims, a business becomes a very valuable contributor to society.

That ranking was my philosophy as CEO and chairman of H.B. Fuller Co., and was typical of the thinking of many Minnesota business owners in years past. They were very generous in their gifts and their work to improve the quality of life in this state. I alluded to one who was a tremendously powerful moving force in Minnesota society—Judson "Sandy" Bemis—when I spoke to the University of Minnesota School of Management's Business Day in 1966.

Since then, we've had a managerial revolution. Instead of businesses being run by their owners, they are run by professional managers. These managers are itinerants, coming and going after only a few years, aiming to enrich themselves as much as possible while they are here. Too often, they don't realize the important role they can play and should play in the development of the community. Sadly, we have seen too many businesses that grew up here successfully, then were taken over or sold and ceased to be the backers of the community that they were when the owners were the managers. This is a trend that, in the long run, will be bad both for business and for Minnesota.

Here is some of what I said about business and society in 1966 – a time when business was part of "the establishment" that was coming in for criticism on college campuses all over the country:

⏭ When I was a student, we were trying to think up a new student award. We wanted to pick something other than a gold cup. We picked a tomato can. Maybe the protest against gross materialism isn't so brand new after all. Yet rebellion is characteristic of our day. Many people are tremendously concerned, and with good reason, about some of the manifestations of rebellion on college campuses around the country. But to me, this is a fundamentally hopeful sign. What it basically means is that there is a re-analysis, a re-appraisal, a pretty healthy skepticism about many of the ideas and the accepted beliefs of the past.

If the ideas, the beliefs and the teachings are sound, they will come out stronger under the withering attack they've been getting on college campuses. If they can't stand it, they will break down and disappear, and maybe they should. Obviously all the expressions, all the methods used in this confrontation are not what some of us would most desire. But basically, I think there is something good going on.

One of the aspects of it, which I think can relate to free enterprise and business, is this searching for a deeper meaning, a challenging purpose in life. There is altogether too prevalent an idea that one of the least idealistic pursuits in life is the business career, an activity worthy only of unintelligent, uncultured slaves of Mammon. Just this week during a visit with some college students, I heard one of them referring to a woman member of the faculty of one of our state colleges as a brilliant, talented, knowledgeable, sparkling personality. And she said, "You know what I found out? She's married to a real estate broker. Can you imagine?" See the context? What could be duller, less intellectual, less sparkling than to be a real estate broker?

We have a businessman in Minnesota who happens to be a bag manufacturer [Judson Bemis]. That is a prosaic, pretty dull sort of a thing to do. You might think, he would have to be a clod to spend his life making bags. Do you know he also happens to be the president of the Minnesota Orchestral Association? He is a great citizen. He has testified before committees of the legislature (on fair employment practices) when it took fearless courage in his own business community to take the stand he took. He is a bag manufacturer, but also he is a great man and a cultured and sparkling personality. There are many like him.

I would suggest two things. One to the students: you can find meaning, purpose, idealism and constructive contribution in a business career. And to the business representatives here, including myself: We need to do a much better job of interpreting what free enterprise really is and does in this country.

No industry group on earth does better at interpreting the qualities of a product and its desirability to potential customers than we do as American business people. You pick up a trade journal or a newspaper in England, for example, and (no offense meant to the wonderful people of England) you read some of their ads, and you can't help but wonder how the people buy anything over there. Skillful communication and creation of desire is a benchmark of achievement of American industry. Yet this same group of fine people fails miserably in interpreting its own role in society.

The role of business has been too often portrayed as solely "to make a profit." Really, we should begin to shift our emphasis toward the real purpose of a business, which is to render a service or to supply a product. If it is a good product and if it is a good service and if the elements that go into making the business a successful enterprise for supplying that product or service are properly managed, there will be a profit.

Business in the United States doesn't have to change so much of what it is doing. It is socially conscious. Business leaders are participating in all manner of community activity. Business contributes mightily to every worthy cause in this land. It is a marvel to the other countries of the world. The voluntary contribution idea is a part of our national scene, not common to other countries. All citizens participate in this. But if you have ever been involved in any kind of a financial drive whatever, you know that a pretty substantial portion of it must come from a relatively small number of contributors, and many of these are corporations, or foundations, or agencies that spring out of corporations. But we businessmen need to put a greater emphasis on philanthropy, to establish the priority in our own minds as to what we really are up to.

Free enterprise has let itself get into a context that somehow makes it appear to be at odds with the public interest, when in fact it is basic to the public interest. No industry group on earth does better at interpreting the qualities of a product and its desirability to potential customers than we do as American business people. You pick up a trade journal or a newspaper in England, for example, and—no offense meant to the wonderful people of England—you read some of their ads, and you can't help but wonder how the people buy anything over there. Skillful communication and creation of desire is a benchmark of achievement of American industry. Yet this same group of fine people fails miserably in interpreting its own role in society.

The role of business has been too often portrayed as solely "to make a profit." Really, we should begin to shift our emphasis toward the real purpose of a business, which is to render a service or to supply a product. If it is a good product and if it is a good service and if the elements that go into making the business a successful enterprise for supplying that product or service are properly managed, there will be a profit.

Business in the United States doesn't have to change so much of what it is doing. It is socially conscious. Business leaders are participating in all manner of community activity. Business contributes mightily to every worthy cause in this land. It is a marvel to the other countries of the world. The voluntary contribution idea is a part of our national scene, not common to other countries. All citizens participate in this. But if you have ever been involved in any kind of a financial drive whatever, you know that a pretty substantial portion of it must come from a relatively small number of contributors, and many of these are corporations, or foundations, or agencies that spring out of corporations. But we businessmen need to put a greater emphasis on philanthropy, to establish the priority in our own minds as to what we really are up to.

Free enterprise has let itself get into a context that somehow makes it appear to be at odds with the public interest, when in fact it is basic to the public interest. Business isn't alone. Government is required.

Business couldn't exist without stable government. You can think of countries with great resources of raw materials, fine people, and seemingly all the elements that ought to produce a prosperous society; but they do not. Why not? Because capital cannot be invested safely—there isn't stable government. You just cannot generate the kind of enterprise that builds a prosperous society—with all the food, equipment, and supplies that are needed—without stability of government. Government is not at odds with industry. It is essential; it is prior. Government doesn't persecute industry. Government exists so people can go into business with the confidence of a secure social situation and an objective legal situation. I believe we need to understand this—that industry is benefited by government. It is a privilege to be in business in the United States of America, under the concept of government we have.

My feeling has been that in our country, when government has encroached on the right of an individual or when government has imposed regimentation of industry, it hasn't come because of any conspiracy. It has come through default, sometimes by business, and sometimes by volunteer organizations in meeting their responsibilities.

We are a free country; we can continue to be free; we can continue to mold the kind of government that we will. Sometimes we mold it by action; but more often in our country, government is molded by inaction.

Some people feel they can choose whether or not they will be involved in messy politics. I think the best illustration of the role of every citizen in our country is that of passing constitutional amendments in the state of Minnesota. The legislature makes the proposal and submits it to the people for ratification. People vote on it in a general election. It takes a majority of all the people who vote at the election to adopt it, not just a majority of those who vote on the issue. Some people walk into the polling booth, and they read the fine print on the constitutional amendment. Then they say to themselves, "I don't really understand this. I don't think I'll vote on it." Their non-vote is recorded as "no." You can vote as strongly through inaction in government as through action.

Business people and all other citizens have a responsibility for participation—as citizens concerned with the public interest, not as representatives of a special interest.

In our country, you don't determine whether or not you are going to participate. It is in the nature of the organization of our government that every adult citizen participates. The only thing you decide is the expression of your participation. Are you going to be casting your vote through inaction, or positive participation?

—May 18, 1966

ELECTRONICS, MINNESOTA STYLE

A governor has a great opportunity to make connections with industries in the state, and determine how state services, laws and regulations might help them flourish. It was with that in mind that my friend and economic development commissioner, Tom Swain, arranged for me a tour of the young, fast-growing Minnesota electronics industry in 1962. The remarks that follow were delivered at the dinner that concluded the two-day experience.

I felt then that this industry had a great future, and I would say today it has an even greater future. But in any new industry, the participants and the role they play change. That has certainly occurred in electronics industry in the past forty years. Honeywell is no longer headquartered in Minnesota. Cray Research, which was an important contributor, is gone. Medtronic, which was so promising when the speech was made in 1962, is still flourishing and growing stronger by the week, with new developments that are unbelievable in their potential. I've read recently about bio-technics, the application of computer science and technology to medical uses. It picks up on Medtronic's pacemaker idea and applies it to hookups to different parts of the brain for different purposes. A person who was having extreme tremors as a result of Parkinson's disease had a plate put in his brain close to the area that affects movement, with a little battery in his chest and a wire running from his brain to his chest, where there was a pacemaker. It reduced his tremor, almost completely eliminating it. There are many other applications where electronics and medicine intersect, providing new miracles of recovery and easing of pain. Such innovation is what makes electronics still a very rich field.

Minnesota's investment in education and turning out qualified students to staff these companies is of the greatest importance. As I said forty years ago, the single most important factor in the growth of the electronics industry has been the University of Minnesota. Investment in the university, in both its faculty and its research facilities, is essential to the type of research that can benefit an industry on the cutting edge of development.

I would also underscore today the necessity of protecting and enhancing the quality of life in Minnesota, if we are to keep this industry thriving here. People who work in the electronics industry command high salaries. They can choose where they wish to live because their services are in demand in many places. Minnesota does much to aid its electronics industry when it invests in the arts, recreation, and professional sports. Those amenities go into making Minnesota a desirable place to live. Here is some of what I said about that in 1962:

⏭ Today, and yesterday too, have been inspiring days. I wish it had been possible for the other 3,900,000 Minnesotans to have been with me. How I would have liked them to have seen the things that I have seen! Yesterday and today, I saw tomorrow. This is a privilege reserved for very few men.

In this room tonight are the architects of tomorrow. Since we have gathered here to salute tomorrow, I wish to pay tribute to these architects whose vision, courage, and imagination this nation and this state sorely need.

For the past two days we have visited the fastest-growing industry in Minnesota, the electronics industry. Tonight we are talking about this industry, which sells $700 million worth of products each year and employs 60,000 of our fellow citizens. We are talking about the fourth largest electronics center in our nation.

I can't tell all of you how grateful I am to find that the University of Minnesota, my own university, is so closely identified with Minnesota's electronics industry. It is heartening to meet corporation executives who, with a deep sense of appreciation, tell me that they are in business in Minnesota because of our university.

Dr. William G. Shepherd, head of the department of electrical engineering at the university, and his colleagues have the warm admiration of a great industry and of informed citizens throughout the state. You, Dr. Shepherd, take your rightful place—you and your associates—among a large group of illustrious university teachers, research scientists and administrators; professors who have given the world the Latham raspberry, blue cheese, taconite the Haralson apple, open heart surgery, the Ring test in brucellosis control—the list is too long. But any listing of their contributions must include reference to those yearly graduating classes of Minnesota boys and girls – young scientists, physicists, veterinarians, social workers, journalists, economists, surgeons, zoologists -- specialists in all of the skills and competences demanded by the unlimited horizons of the society we have created.

To those who believe that the university is too big, may I call attention to the fact that the university is not big enough for the electronics industry. This electronics industry is not a muscle industry, it is a brain industry. Last year, five—only five—out of the 150 electronics companies in Minnesota hired three times as many electrical engineers as the university graduated. This year, one of these five companies alone will employ as many electrical engineers as the university will graduate. Small wonder that the field of electrical engineering is the fastest growing one in the university's graduate school!

I would be remiss, indeed, if I did not make reference to the excellent Minnesota vocational schools which teach trades indigenous to the electronics industry. I would be remiss if I did not call attention to Minnesota's apprenticeship training programs, perhaps the best in the nation, some of which are related to the manpower needs of this industry.

We can be proud that our state offers cultural educational and recreational advantages of a high order, particularly attractive to the young industries represented in this room and to their young scientists, engineers, administrators, and craftsmen and their families. Museums, a great symphony orchestra, excellent libraries, public and private elementary, secondary and higher education facilities of the highest quality, art centers, theaters, churches of many creeds and faiths, unequalled outdoor recreational opportunities, concert and lecture programs, big league athletics, newspapers and radio and television stations that are nationally recognized as great—all these become important to those identified with the kind of industry with which we are dealing. As we seek to become the Detroit of the electronics industry, which is our goal, these great educational, cultural and recreational offerings are invaluable.

Let there be no mistake about it, the people of Minnesota are proud of all that is represented in this hall tonight. A part of Minnesota—a part of the brain and the competence of Minnesota—went with Colonel [John] Glenn in his three orbits of our world, and in this same way, parts of Minnesota are in the Polaris program; they are in the ICBM systems; they are in all high-altitude work involving the cosmic rays; they are in technical systems and in defense programs. We are proud of Minnesota's contributions that relate to the outer space frontiers of tomorrow, to the defense and the protection of a civilization and a way of life.

Our earnest hope is that we in Minnesota may rise to the great occasions of which we are so much a part; that we may meet today each of the demands of tomorrow. In this I have a compelling responsibility as governor. I share this responsibility with every state official, with every member of the legislature, with every member of the bench, with all citizens who are concerned with our state, with its laws, its patterns, and its rates of growth. I know I speak for the entire state, and for the citizens which make up our communities, when I pledge enthusiastic support to Minnesota's electronics industry and wish it well in the years ahead.

We urge deliberate speed in launching an Upper Midwest Research Institute. This will be another key factor in continuing the dynamic growth of technically oriented industry. It is greatly to the credit of our Minnesota people that they have supplied large amounts of venture capital to new companies organized here. The Twin Cities market in new securities has been a lively one, and some sensational successes have occurred. That there will be some failures should surprise no one. This is in the nature of speculative enterprise. The development of the auto industry saw many companies formed and a number fail. Those that survived had very great success, as did their stockholders. I am anxious that we encourage Minnesota as a healthy climate for investment in new enterprise. It augurs well for our future when young men of vision and ability build a company around an idea, offer equity shares to the public, and launch new firms in our midst. This has characterized the growth of our electronics industry.

I said I regretted I did not have every Minnesotan along with me today. My, how I wish they had seen Medtronic's "cardiac implantable pacemaker"—that amazing pocket-size ticker which sparks hesitant heart beats and provides added years of near-normal life for many cardiac patients.

The history of this company is the history, more or less, of all such companies. Medtronic started in 1949. It had three people on its payroll then. Its gross sales for its first month amounted to $8; it used 600 square feet of space, in a garage! It has its own building now; new and spic and span. The three employees have grown to forty-six; it's quite a place, you will want to know.

It's quite a jump from Medtronic, which incidentally is not the smallest of the electronic concerns in Minnesota, to the Minneapolis Honeywell Company, which is Minnesota's largest. Operating almost everywhere, it employs more than 45,000 persons and more than one-third of these are working right here in Minnesota. Its payroll now is on the order of one hundred million dollars. We are happy to share with the free world the competence of this great Minnesota organization, and tonight we particularly salute its electronic operations relating to missiles, space vehicles, aircraft, and so on. We were there too today.

At Remington Rand Univac in St. Paul, we saw evidence of the great growth and vitality so typical of this industry. With a payroll covering 6,000 persons, St. Paul Univac is now the third largest private employer in the Twin Cities area. Its operations make it Minnesota's largest computer manufacturer. Merchants, farmers, the folks who take up the church collections, waitresses, bankers, taxicab drivers, and a lot of the rest of us, are grateful for its $35 million annual payroll. Six hundred Minnesota suppliers do business with Univac.

At Control Data, with 1,700 employees, I saw digital computers in operation and learned something about the "Polaris Submarine Mark 84 Fire Control System"—not much, but enough to have a faint comprehension of the indebtedness of the free world to Minneapolis' Control Data.

At Telex, Inc. I was exposed to "line printers," and to "disc files." At Data Display I saw things that I hope you won't ask me to explain—impressive things used in military data systems and satellite control centers. At Magnetic Controls Company, with four plants in St. Louis Park, two in St. Peter and one in Southern California, I got a glimpse of automation, the use of electronics systems in the mixing of things like concrete, livestock feeds and bread dough.

Electronics are big in Minnesota, and they'll be bigger. We're growing at an increasing rate, and that produces the prettiest economic graph there is.

—March 9, 1962

REPORT TO LABOR

Politicians today seem to spend a great deal of campaign time and energy appealing to voters who already share their views. I always liked to reach beyond my Republican base, even to voters who were plainly loyal to the Democratic-Farmer-Labor Party. I thought I could offer them something positive, and I was not easily dissuaded by an initially cool reception.

It was in that spirit that I invited myself to the state AFL-CIO convention in Rochester about six weeks before the 1962 election. Labor was, and is, very pro-DFL. I called the AFL-CIO officials and said that, as governor, I wanted to give them a report. My administration had a strong industrial record, and I knew I was making inroads among rank-and-file union voters.

My goal that day in Rochester was as much to win support for what was called the Taconite Amendment as it was for my own reelection. I had such strong feeling about the proposed constitutional amendment, and wanted the 1963 legislature to put it on the ballot in 1964. The amendment assured investors in taconite plants on Minnesota's Iron Range of fair, stable taxation, the same as any other business could expect. It ended the practice of separate, often heavy-handed taxation of the mining industry. The taconite industry was in its infancy in Minnesota in the 1960s. The nation's steel companies were reluctant to invest in Minnesota plants unless the state was willing to promise them even-handed tax treatment. I couldn't understand why organized labor, which had so much to gain from development of Minnesota's taconite industry, would oppose the Taconite Amendment. It was so obvious that the Iron Range would wither economically if we didn't do something, and that the gain could be tremendous if we took some action. There were some union officials in northeastern Minnesota who were so died-in-the-wool Democratic that they were against anything a Republican offered. And there were some in the Twin Cities who did not appreciate the fact that H.B. Fuller employees felt no need for a union.

Labor came around on the Taconite Amendment, but not until after the 1962 election. They then brought my DFL opponent and successor as governor, Karl Rolvaag, around to supporting the amendment too. I kept working on its passage after I left office. It was overwhelmingly approved by the voters in 1964, and the taconite industry blossomed as a result.

Unfortunately, the years of sustained prosperity that taconite brought the Iron Range seem to be coming to an end. If I were governor today, I would make a study of the modernization of steel plants, and work out a cooperative arrangement between industry and government to finance a modernization effort. The U.S. steel industry has not kept pace, and technology in Japan and other countries has improved so they can import ore and coal, produce steel and sell it in the United States under our cost. Investment in technological improvement is needed, and may require some state assistance. The once-mighty American steel industry is sick right now, and needs help to survive.

My remarks at the 1962 state labor convention received lukewarm applause, nothing more. Here is some of what I said:

⏭ I come to Rochester as one who, twenty months ago, raised his hand and swore to administer fairly and without prejudice an office that exists to serve all the people. I come as a friend of labor. I speak as governor, determined that the labor movement shall not be denied the official greeting from our citizens that only a governor can bring. Our people support the aims of the labor movement and wish your convention well. I join them and extend a personal wish for a productive and constructive convention.

I am glad that I can report that, except for northeastern Minnesota, employment conditions in our state are excellent. Employment is up by 265,000 jobs from January 1961 to August 1962, a rate of increase three times the national average for the same period.

Unemployment, even including the difficult northeastern Minnesota situation, is down to 3.8 per cent, a figure below the 4 percent goal President Kennedy has set for the country, which still registers 5.3 percent unemployment overall. Also, very importantly, Minnesota's per capita income is currently growing at twice the national rate of increase. To have employment and per capita personal income both rising in our state at a rate substantially above the national average is the best economic news any governor could bring to a convention of representatives of working people.

I feel it is vital that we work together to build a greater Minnesota. It is important for our working people to know that in their governor they have a champion, and that I will cooperate in every way with their labor organizations when the efforts and energies of those organizations are directed at improving the lot of the working man.

It would not be candid to say that there had been no differences of opinion between some of labor's leaders and me on the subject of long-range assurance of tax fairness for taconite. The issue affects labor as no other issue has in many years in Minnesota. It has implications not only in economics, but also in individual rights. I maintain that it is the right of the people of Minnesota to decide, at the polls, whether or not such assurance should be granted.

There are those within the body of labor who say that there should be assurance, and that it should be provided by statute [rather than constitutional amendment.] With them I disagree only in form, method, and effectiveness. But there have been those, notably the leaders of the steelworkers, who passed a resolution opposing assurances, whether by statute or amendment. I am convinced that if this attitude should prevail, it would sound an economic death knell for jobs and opportunities in northeastern Minnesota. With them my disagreement is total. To me it is unthinkable that such a reactionary approach should succeed in preventing the location of taconite plants and taconite jobs in Minnesota. It is unthinkable that this attitude should not only deprive the people of Minnesota of the opportunity to vote on a measure that is to their long-term benefit, but also that reprisals should be threatened against those who believe in either the amendment or statutory approach.

I am not alone in this view. As one example, Fred Cina, Liberal Majority Leader of the House of Representatives, said on September 10 just past, that "firm determined action" is needed to attract more taconite plants to Minnesota. He is a supporter of a tax guarantee to the taconite industry.

My door is always open to you to discuss this or any other measures. Samuel Gompers once said, "What does labor want? We want more schoolhouses and less jails; more books and less arsenals; more learning and less vice; more leisure and less greed; more justice and less revenge; in fact, more of the opportunities to cultivate our better natures; to make manhood more noble, womanhood more beautiful and childhood more happy and bright." In this I'm with you, all the way.

I extend the best wishes of all our people and thank you for allowing me to appear today. You have been kind and courteous in your attention. I knew you would be.

—September 24, 1962

EARL BAKKEN

I have always admired people who have successful business careers, making themselves self-supporting and responsible, but who do not limit their focus to their business. The really valuable part of a person's life is that which is devoted to the service of others.

Such a man in Minnesota is Earl Bakken, the brilliant electrical engineer who founded Medtronic Corporation in 1949, while he was still a graduate student at the University of Minnesota. Along with Dr. C. Walton Lillehei at the university, he developed the first wearable, transistorized cardiac pacemaker in 1957. I cannot say that I know him well, but our paths have crossed several times through the years. He established the Bakken Library and Museum of Electricity in Life in 1975, and I was honored when he invited me to serve on its board. He currently lives in Hawaii, and has been the moving spirit in the building of a hospital there. We have been a little involved in that project as well.

Here is some of what I said at the dedication of the Bakken Library's acquisition of volumes one to eighty-five of the *Journal De Physique*, the most important scientific journal of the eighteenth century:

⏭ I would like to recall and celebrate what and who has brought us to this point. I well remember receiving a call thirty years ago from Jerry Shepherd of the University of Minnesota telling me of a remarkable invention that had the effect of stimulating and reinforcing heart action where it was failing due to age or disease. He invited me to see a demonstration using a dog as the patient. I shall always remember the sight of that fine healthy dog, full of life and vigor until the pacemaker implant was shut off. Almost immediately he became listless and was obviously failing. Turning the pacemaker on again restored the natural spirit of that animal in moments. It was an incredible demonstration of a remarkable device. That was my first introduction to Medtronic and its founder, Earl Bakken.

Some months later I was invited to the offices of Medtronic by Mr. Bakken to see some of the material in his collection of books and equipment relating to the history of electricity. Once again, I was most impressed. Here was a successful business executive who combined the creativity that builds a successful company with a scholarly interest in books and scientific history, instead of total preoccupation with the corporate bottom line.

It was some time later that I learned he had bought this property, organized a non-profit institution, and launched a most important library and museum. On one visit I had a tour of the library and was tremendously impressed with librarian Elizabeth Ihrig and the meticulously efficient way materials were organized and cataloged.

Mr. Bakken asked Dennis Stillings, the technical librarian at Medtronic, in the 1960s to find "some old medical electrical machines." Stillings found it easier to find early books than machines, but through book dealers, he found his way to sources of the apparatuses Mr. Bakken wanted to acquire. Stillings' experiences, which read like adventure stories, took him to Florida, Mexico and England, and resulted in bringing together a truly remarkable and unique collection to which an important addition is celebrated today.

The Bakken collections now comprise approximately 12,000 books, bound volumes of journals and manuscripts, and close to 2,000 instruments and machines. The focus of the collection is on the historical role of electricity and magnetism in the life sciences. The historian of science, W. D. Hackman, once said of the Bakken Library that one might be able to put together something like it by combining the relevant materials from the libraries at Cambridge, Oxford and Wellcome in England, but that nowhere except at the Bakken Library can one find a single resource of such richness for doing research into the history of medical and experimental uses of electricity in life.

So as we salute and celebrate this institution and its most recent important acquisition, we salute and congratulate Earl Bakken for what he has done for human health and welfare, for scientific knowledge and for the distinction he has brought to the state of Minnesota.

—March 8, 1991

MINNESOTA FARMERS

I am so appreciative of farmers. I used to meet farmers at county fairs. When I would ask a man, "What do you do?" and he would say, "I'm just a farmer," I would say, "Don't say you're *just* a farmer. You're an important guy. Say it with pride and the knowledge that what you do is important to the enterprise of the whole society."

I have great respect for people who appreciate the land, who work with it to use it sparingly, not to use it up, and to restore it. Fundamental to all else in a society is care for the land, the water, and the environment. Without them, society cannot survive.

I am increasingly concerned about how much rich agricultural land is being lost each year, in Minnesota and elsewhere, to urban development. We may be paving over our capacity to feed ourselves. If we must depend on others for our food, we will be in a very dangerous position. I fear that in the long view of history, the decline of the great American nation could someday be attributable to our failure to nurture our natural resources, particularly our farmland.

Farm life has been an important social institution in Minnesota. As a businessman, when I was looking for employees, I tended to favor young people who came off the farm. They had learned cooperation, since a family farm depends on every individual doing his or her share of the work.

They learn habits of responsibility and of steadiness. In our own family, I thought our children should have the experience of farm life, so I bought a dairy farm in 1953. We farmed for thirty-five years. I wanted the family to have some exposure to working with nature and learning about life from a farm existence. It opens up life to its manifold experiences. To me, the greatest heritage a child can have is farm life.

Those experiences and values were much on my mind as I spoke in 1994 at the occasion of the first annual presentation of the Siehl Prize for Excellence in Agriculture at the University of Minnesota. There were three award-winners that day, Dr. William A. Larson, Bert Enestvedt, and Al Bloomquist. Each of them was on my mind, but so was someone in the audience: Norman Borlaug, the University of Minnesota alumnus who won the Nobel Peace Prize in 1970 for his work increasing the yield capacity of wheat. I considered it a great honor to speak about agriculture with him in attendance. As I often did in later years, I spoke without a text. Here is some of what was captured on tape that day:

⏭ I'm sure all of you realize that this is a very awesome occasion. It deals with reverence for the earth, the land. When the word "land" is even said, it has special connotations to all of us. It's at the heart of all of us. This occasion deals with family solidarity and continuity that makes contributions to seed. A seed, one seed, can represent all of life. This occasion recognizes persons who provide leadership, who take the initiative to do something so that a group of people can take command of their own lives, can take command of their resources, and build a future for themselves and for the state. All of these are noble issues.

I remember, some years ago, meeting a refugee from Europe, Walter Kosteletzy who had been in the country several months. I asked, "Walter, I'm sure there must be several impressions you have of the United States. What really impresses you the most?" He paused, then said, "I think what impresses me the most in the United States is a food store. I wonder if you have any idea what the impact is to come from where I come from and to be able to walk into a great establishment and, limited only by your means, to have access to all varieties and abundance of food—food well prepared, food well packaged, food so delicious. That impresses me the most about the United States." I've thought about that ever since. Sometimes, I think there ought to be a little sign over our grocery stores: "Breathe a prayer of thanks for food."

I often think how unheralded are the people who produce the food that we all enjoy in such abundance. When I think of a tough job, I think of the tough jobs on a farm during the winter. I think of the tough job when a silo unloader is broken in bitterly cold weather when iron can become brittle, steel breakable. I think of it when we have sub-zero mornings. I think of some farmer, somewhere in Minnesota, climbing up the outside of his silo to get up to that top unloader—many of them now are bottom unloaders—and chop loose some silage so the rhythm of regular feeding of a dairy herd will not be interrupted by a breakdown. That's hard work, for which we can never give adequate thanks or adequate recognition. I don't think there is any group of workers in our country who, if they were measured in rates of pay per hour actually employed, would have a lower hourly return for their labor than agricultural workers.

Yet, in that desperately hard work in such a tremendously important industry, they have built fortitude of character, loyalty of family, soundness of values, so that one of the great reputations of any young person going anywhere in the United States is that he grew up on a farm. He grew up on a farm. It means he has habits. It means he has standards. It means he knows how to work. It means that he is an admirable employee for anyone to seek. So, to pay tribute to farmers and farm production is really a tremendous occasion.

Our laureates today impress me so much. It was said of Dr. William Larson that there can be generic principles that are fairly easily understood, but it takes enormous dedication to gather the data, to make the studies, to project the models that give evidence and credibility to a position requiring great attitudinal change by farmers and others. He was one of the first to come up with what we now call conservation tillage as a method of controlling erosion. But that was only the beginning. He went then to get statistical data on the importance of residual crop in the preservation of the soil, to preserve the soil for sustainable agriculture.

When we think of what the population is going to become, there can be true concern. Are we going to be able to feed all of the people? If we erode the soil, if we destroy the source of food, there won't be. Dr. Larson, in one area after another, was on the cutting edge of new developments, studying the mechanics of soil, the mechanics of soil compression and compaction, and the quantification of product-specific soils of the world, so that we can know where is the soil most suitable for which product with the minimum of chemical treatment and the minimal drain on the soil's future productivity. Dr. Larson has produced paper after paper of statistical analysis, more recently computerized projections, 250 publications over a period of 37 years. I'd say that's awesome. A hundred years from now, if the people of this world are being fed, a good deal of the reason will be the work of Dr. William A. Larson.

The Enestvedt family has been important in Minnesota for ninety-four years. It was 1900 when Bert's father started the family's original farm. He was one of the early persons in the Minnesota Crop Improvement Association. That was one of the early efforts in the country to develop better seed varieties. When Bert came along he became very active in hybridization. The whole Enestvedt family has been in this enterprise, so there's a value, a humanistic value, in that family working together for all these years, taking pride in the standard, in the integrity, in the quality of what they were doing, so that 60 percent of the certified seed produced on the Enestvedt farm is sold in the immediate area to friends and neighbors, people who rely on the Enestvedt standard. To have that honored is certainly honoring ourselves.

I love coming to Al Bloomquist. We who have been in government frequently tell people, "Write and tell your legislators what you think about things. Write in your own way, from your own experience and, believe us, it will be heard." American Crystal Sugar was losing ground in the Red River Valley. One of the four plants had been closed. Farmers of the Red River Valley who depended on sugar beets were in decline. It was a serious situation. So Al Bloomquist wrote a letter. He wrote a letter to the president of American Crystal Sugar. He asked, if a group of growers could be put together and the finances could be raised, would they consider selling? Somewhat to his surprise, the answer came back, "Yes, we would." The growers were put together, the finances were arranged. I'm sure there were some naysayers—there always are—but, leadership prevailed. The deal was made. American Crystal Sugar Cooperative was formed, the first sugar beet producing cooperative in the country, and it succeeded. I think it's a wonderful American saga of a group of growers taking their lives in their own hands, taking their resources under their own control, and building a success.

I don't think any people in the country could surpass the three being honored today in the quality, the integrity, the importance of their work and the leadership of their personalities. To write a letter about something you believe in; to maintain a standard of excellence and integrity whatever your work may be; to have the perseverance and dedication that you can spend a lifetime persuading people what they really ought to know—that we must preserve the soil or someday, we'll not be preserved ourselves. I think this is a reverent occasion, because it gets to the values that are at the center of our very lives and well-being. What a thrill for all of us that we can participate.

—March 17, 1994

STEELWORKERS

I have a strong feeling for northeastern Minnesota, even though not many people in that Democratic region voted for me. I like the region very much for its lovable people. They are straightforward, honest, loyal and self-reliant. As governor, I wanted to try to secure for them the benefits of a more stable economy. This speech, given extemporaneously in 1962 and captured on tape, reflects that desire.

I called then for a dose of trade protectionism, which was considered good policy at the time. Now, forty years later, the world has changed. We have to think in world terms, of the rights and needs of people elsewhere than in our own country. We've become a hated country. People have shown that they are willing to give up their own lives to attack us. Something needs to be done about that, other than retribution. Our own security depends on discovering a way to extend prosperity everywhere. Free trade is increasingly thought to be the best answer. Our security depends not on our military defense, but on a policy of concern for other people.

American companies sometimes contend that they must move their operations overseas to escape this country's high wages or environmental regulations. I have always considered those arguments misguided. Would Americans want to subject themselves and their employees to health-threatening air pollution, as has existed at times in parts of Eastern Europe and the former Soviet Union? High wages and high productivity usually go hand-in-hand. Where wages are high, as in Minnesota, the quality of work performed is high as well. I remember so well the Ford Motor Company president saying that the Ford plant in St. Paul was the most efficient plant in the whole Ford empire. I've never felt that the low wages of undeveloped countries offered a great advantage.

Just as industry promoted education decades ago, in the early stages of worker development, now it must invest in national stability by investing in the creation of good lives for all people. That is the trade argument I would make today. Here is a portion of the transcript of what I said in 1962, at Duluth's VFW Club Post 1217, to members of the United Steelworkers Local 1028:

⏭ I'd like to tell you a little bit about myself and where I came from. Some people think of me as some kind of a bigshot. The fact of the matter is that I came out of a workingman's family. My dad was born in Norway and he came over here as a young fellow just as a lot of other people did, and he settled in Chicago and became a streetcar motorman. My earliest memory is riding with him up in front of the streetcar on Halsted Street in Chicago. When we'd get to the cross streets he'd tell me, "Elmer, you can bang the bell." Then I'd bang the bell down on the floor.

We moved to Muskegon, Michigan, when I was very young. I had two older brothers and a younger sister. When I was fourteen, we lost both of our parents in the same year, some months apart. We four children stayed together and kept house together.

The fact of the matter is for the first several months after this happened, I was kind of chief cook and bottle washer for the family—my two older brothers worked, and then we began to get reorganized. The two older brothers went back to high school and they got through high school. We had this strong feeling in us, as I know your folks put into you, that you should get an education. We worked together and all four children went through high school, went on through college. We helped each other. They all stayed over in Michigan. When I got through junior college in Michigan, the company that I had been working for since I was 14 sent me up to Minnesota to represent them. This brought me here. Then I went to the University, met my wife, and have been here ever since.

In 1934, wanting to get away from constant traveling because we were married and looking forward to a family, I went to work for a firm called H.B. Fuller Company in St. Paul. They manufacture adhesives, pastes and glues for packaging. You walk through a grocery story and all the labels are fastened to packages, and that's the kind of stuff they make. I was on the inside end of promotion and advertising and so on.

Just to be very brief about it, in 1939, Mr. Fuller, who was the president and majority stockholder in this little company, had a stroke. A couple of years later when his recovery was pretty slow, he decided he was going to sell. After some offers from outside companies, we made a little contract and my wife and I scraped the down payment and bought a majority interest in this company, which at that time had annual sales of $200,000. Then I became the president of H.B. Fuller Company in 1941. We worked like the dickens ever since and tried to follow a pattern of operation that encouraged growth, and I continued as the president until I left to take my new job.

I would like to tell you quickly just some of the provisions in our plants to give you some idea of what my attitude is toward a workingman. In the first place, the whole idea of the Fuller Company was that the primary concern was towards the customer. You just have to have customers and take good care of them or no one gets anything. But, second only to that, the responsibility of our company was toward the people who worked there. These people were associated together and we tried in every way we could to show this. We never had a union. We were never organized. Just never came about. But, anyway, we did some of these things:

In the first place, we had Blue Shield and Blue Cross paid for in total by the company, and with the later provision that when people retired at the age of sixty-five, the Blue Cross and Blue Shield protection goes on as long as they live, at the expense of the company. In 1945 we instituted a retirement income plan that combined retirement income and insurance, and this was wholly paid for by the company. Then, when we felt we couldn't increase the annual premiums we were paying on the retirement income, we cast about for some other way to add to the security of our people. We started a profit-sharing trust. At the start of every year, 15 percent of the net profit went into this trust for the benefit of all of the employees in the exact proportion that their income was to the total income of everybody in the place. Everybody in that way was on the same basis, from top to bottom. Another provision was that after ten years of service, if they left, they could take the cash value of this profit-sharing trust with them. We have ten days of annual sick leave. And this accumulates indefinitely. There again, it is up to the individual. If he's absent due to illness, he just tells his supervisor. He gets his full pay.

I just want you to know that I came up through the ranks from a modest immigrant family. I worked fifty-four hours a week, twenty-five cents an hour, and I was never as pleased as one summer when they put me on piecework, and I really went to town. I will never forget, no matter what other checks I ever see, a check that I brought home for two weeks' pay of about fifty-four dollars. So, I just want you to know that I have worked in a plant as a workman, all the way through.

Now to go specifically to American Steel and Wire—what some of the problems are, how they relate to other problems, and what we can do about them. The one fact to recognize, of course, is that the only way that any company can succeed is to produce something that somebody will buy, at a price that will keep the place going and keep it replenished with machinery and equipment. The only thing that is going to keep this mill going is to be able to have a market for enough of its products at a price at which they can be sold.

Here are some of the things that have been happening: In the first place, we do have the problem of imported steel and steel products, and this is tough competition. It used to be true that we could out-produce the rest of the world because we had more modern equipment. But as part of our country's interest in helping other countries to build up, we have provided them with steel plants in Germany that were made with United States funds under the Marshall Plan, and they are more modern than the American Steel and Wire mill here in West Duluth. So this is tough competition, and we have to work out these relationships. I don't believe that the answer is to shut it all off and live unto ourselves. We have to work out a balanced relationship with the rest of the world.

While we are working on these reciprocal agreements, I think we have to protect our own people during the adjustment. After I became governor, I became aware that on the highways of our state, wire fabric mesh used for reinforcing in concrete highways was coming into Minnesota from overseas. I thought it was just too much to expect people here in West Duluth to be working short hours, ready to produce something for our public highways, and then have it coming in from England or Germany. So, beginning in March of 1961, we wrote into the highway department specifications that all steel must be of domestic production. This was the first time this had been done.

Another way to have more markets right now would be to accelerate our highway production program, just on a kind of a public works basis. It would help if the federal government would catch up on its payments to us. One thing about the interstate program that is not understood is that there are two parts to federal participation. They pay 90 percent; the state government pays 10. They announced allocations of money to Minnesota, but they don't pay those allocations until they're approved by the budget bureau. Congress can allocate money, but you can't actually spend it until they've got it in hand and say that you can spend it. I mention that because the fact of the matter is, the federal government is $78 million dollars behind in actually providing us with the money that has been allocated to us.

Another market for products of American Steel and Wire is in the field of agriculture. You make—of course, you know far better than I—all manner of agricultural products, barbed wire fence and so on. So what we are doing in agriculture in Minnesota is of importance. The whole effort there in this administration is to try and find the specialty products that Minnesota can produce to advantage, that someone wants to buy, that we can sell at a profit, and keep our farms producing. When farms go out of production and go into the soil bank, it sure hits the fence post, barbed-wire fencing and other farm supply industries right in the head. If there is any way that we can keep these industries going, and agriculture going, we want to do it.

I understand you've had splendid relationships with your local management. And I'm just as sure as anything that there's nothing they'd rather see more than this plant be modernized and flourish and prosper. And if you, between yourselves, in the plant, could work up a committee to go down to Cleveland to meet with the top management in the American Steel and Wire Division of U. S. Steel, and you wanted me to go with you, I'd be glad to go along, just to discuss what we can do by working together. What do you need to modernize this plant and make it a continuing, prospering agency? What can we do to help?

—March 25, 1962

THE ESSENCE OF POLITICS

When I talk to business groups, I like to work in an encouragement for them to participate in politics. There has always been a feeling among some business people that they can't engage in politics, because it would mean siding with a party that represented only a portion of their customers, and that the others would take offense. Business people want everybody to love them! I would tell them that if a businessman put a banner across his place of business reading, "I am a Republican" or "I am a Democrat," and then ran a good business with good values and good service, the words on that banner would not make a bit of difference. People don't care about politics when they're shopping.

I advise business people to participate firsthand in democracy. When they hire lobbyists or delegate their representation to a business association, they should be sure to know what is being said in their name or on their behalf. I've known splendid businessmen who were ruthlessly represented in the legislature, and would have been appalled at the tactics employed.

The best business people understand that measures giving them an advantage at the expense of others are not healthy in the long run. In our economy, as well as our democracy, those who seek advantage must always think about its effect on all of the people. If the people lose, eventually, so will business.

Some business people shun political involvement for another reason. As long as their role is making financial contributions, they are treated royally in political circles. But as soon as they attempt to have some influence, a struggle begins between what they believe and what others believe. Engaging in that struggle seems unattractive to some people. I found that participating in debate over public policy is healthy. It's interesting. It's enlivening. You make good friends, and you sharpen your own wits in the process. To recognize there are two sides to an issue, to study the points and arrive at a viewpoint, to know both sides and respect them, but then choose your own stand and be willing to fight for it, that's American citizenship.

My habit of speaking to groups without notes or a text had a downside: When someone asked afterwards for a copy of some portion of my remarks, I either had to disappoint that interested listener, or improvise. What follows is the rather terse product of one such improvisation, after a speech in the 1950s to a Chamber of Commerce group. Here is my brief, post-speech summation of that point, which I titled "The Essence of Politics":

⏭ Participation in politics is different in one key respect from activity in many other fields. Politics is essentially a struggle for power to see who is going to hold party or public office, and what ideas or programs are going to prevail in party platforms, and in governmental action. Constantly, in politics, then, one is fighting for whom he supports, or what he believes, against resistance and opposition.

In your service club, fraternal organization, or social group, you are sought out and asked to do things, and your help is welcomed. In politics you may not be invited, indeed, you may not be wanted, and your suggestions and participation may be resisted. To go into politics, you must have beliefs or purpose for which you are willing to fight.

IV. EDUCATION

WHAT TEACHERS GIVE TO US

Public education has been a great positive force in the development of the United States. A strong emphasis on education is the secret to securing this nation's future. My support for public education has, if anything, grown stronger in the years since I served in elective office. As family influence has declined in so many children's lives, society relies ever more on schools to prepare the next generation for responsible citizenship.

Too much cannot be said for the need to adequately reach every student with the knowledge and values that citizenship requires. With Minnesota's more and more diverse population, we need more and more diverse forms of education. Education is an individual process, and there has to be great variability of program to truly meet the learning and social needs of every young person.

I would add a word about an education funding question being debated currently, the proposal for tax-provided vouchers for paying private school tuition. I do not favor vouchers. Private education meets a need, particularly for people who want religious influence coupled with education. But to subtract funds from public education through a voucher system, in my opinion, goes the wrong way. Tax dollars should be used to make public education the best it can be.

This is what I said about education, and about the important role that teachers play, to the Minnesota Education Association's summer meeting in 1959:

⏭ I wonder: Do you understand how overwhelming your influence can be on the young people who come to you each year? My guess is that few teachers appreciate the extent of their reach into young lives. Chance remarks they make may stay with a child for life. Efforts to communicate over the resistance of indifference may have an impact beyond all recognition at the time. In my life, as in many, teachers have been the greatest influence except for my parents. Often, I reflect on particular teachers and what they meant to me.

I was born in Chicago, but when I was very young the family moved to Muskegon, Michigan, where I attended the elementary grades, high school, and junior college. My first teacher recollection is of Miss Ione Williams. I suffered an attack of polio when I was nine years old. I was bed-ridden for a time, but gradually strength returned until I could walk. At this point, I returned to school. Even then, if I should trip and fall, it was necessary to get to some support, where I could pull myself up, as my arms were stronger than my legs. Sometimes pulling myself up meant crawling to a nearby fence or tree. Every movement and effort was exercise that aided in restoring strength. Possibly on instruction, I do not know, Miss Williams let me struggle with my walking, let me pull myself up when necessary, never aided me to rise when I fell, and must have urged this restraint upon others. She permitted me to fight back for strength and to learn self-reliance.

I am sure she must have suffered more than I did. The restraint she exercised could not have been easy. This was brought home to me a few years ago in connection with a legislative interim commission study of handicapped children. We were visiting a class of cerebral palsy children who were learning to walk. Before we entered the room, we were told that we would see children struggling very hard to walk and that some might fall—and that we would almost instinctively want to help them up. However, we were directed not to do this, as it would weaken rather than help the children. We entered the room, and it certainly was a moving experience to see these young folks with unresponsive bodies going through an excruciating struggle to walk. Sure enough, one of the youngsters fell, and we could hardly stand to watch as that youngster raised himself back on his feet to struggle on. Nearby were children in more advanced stages of training, and these were an inspiration to the beginners. As I watched, my mind went back to Miss Williams, and more than ever before, I wished I could then say a word of thanks for a teacher who let me learn lessons that one can only learn for himself. I am sure it takes greater maturity, wisdom and patience to let a child learn with effort for himself, than to be over-aided to a successful accomplishment.

Miss Mabel Seeley was a junior high teacher who later became a principal. I do not remember what she told the class but I shall never forget what she told me. To her, I was a particular individual who had her personal attention. Miss Seeley had a great capacity for love of her children and life in general. She was a robust person who smiled easily, laughed heartily and encouraged people around her to relax and let go. Hers was a wholesome, outgoing personality. I felt her love for me, and must have responded like a grateful puppy. I must have been pretty thin and weak looking, because I was one of several who had milk in the afternoon and took bed rest in her office. It was our chance to talk.

Two screech owls were discovered in the bell tower of our old-fashioned school. Some of the boys pelted stones at them until the janitor put a stop to it and called Miss Seeley to the scene. She directed the rescue operation of the battered pair, and then let me take them home to nurse back to health. I loved the job; the owls responded and soon were released. This fed my interest in nature study, bird watching, butterfly collecting, aquarium keeping, ant colonies in mason jars, all supplemented with readings that Miss Seeley provided.

I seemed to live in a special world with Miss Seeley. Near her home was a cherry orchard owned by a friend of hers. She got me a job cherry-picking and after work, before going home, I would stop and visit her. We would chat about many subjects. She once drew me out on the topic of the origin of earth and man, and I may have expressed some very fundamentalist, arbitrary ideas. I remember so well how she mused over what I said, making no reply for quite a while. I was almost afraid I had hurt her feelings. Finally she said, "Elmer, there are elements of truth in what you say, but some day a greater truth may come to you. Keep your mind open to receive it." How wise and wonderful she was!

Miss Seeley taught me to open my heart to people, she taught me to notice the wonders of nature, she taught me to accept life and enjoy the challenge of living it, and she taught me to always keep my mind open for a greater truth. That was a great deal to teach a young lad—but she was a very great teacher. Her influence has stayed with me through the years since I met her in seventh grade, and the learning she started in me continues. One cannot fully learn all she endeavored to teach; one can only travel along the road of learning.

Miss Caroline Barber was an instructor in English literature at our junior college. My vision of Miss Barber is as she stood before the class, working herself into a lather as she told of Robert Browning or as she read from Byron, Shelley and Keats. She would get so excited that she would literally not hear the closing bell, and when informed that the period was over, she would almost collapse with frustration at so little material covered. At first, we students, all in our late teens, thought she was a nut. Gradually, however, it penetrated our somewhat unresponsive attitudes that she was a sincere, dedicated person who believed in her work intensely. She knew that what Browning said was important, and that Keats had written some of the most beautiful lines in all literature. By sheer force of her personality and enthusiasm, English literature became alive. To me, she is the personification of communication as opposed to mere presentation. She not only presented, she transmitted. She reached us and captured our minds and imagination in a way that could not help but have great impact. My own love of books and reading started there. I shall never forget her discussion of the significance of Browning's line, "A man's reach should exceed his grasp, or what is a heaven for?"

Last year, I met Maria Sanford. She is the teacher Minnesotans chose to honor by having her statue placed in the national Capitol in Washington as one of but two Minnesotans to be so recognized. I met her through Helen Whitney's biography, but more especially through people who knew her and were her students. I will permit myself but one illustration from her life and work. When Maria Sanford lived in southeast Minneapolis, she had some apple trees in her yard that were her pride and joy. You can imagine her dismay, when she came out one fall morning and found that her trees had been looted the night before. Without too much effort, she singled out the half-dozen neighborhood boys who were responsible. What would be a good pedagogical approach to such a situation? Miss Sanford went down to a nursery and bought six apple trees, hunted up the boys, marched from the yard of one to the yard of another and at each stop presented and helped plant an apple tree. I doubt that any of those boys could ever forget the significance of that experience. Miss Sanford taught consideration for others and respect for their property.

In paying tribute to these excellent teachers, I mean to direct attention to the qualities that made them great. Your program at this leadership workshop is directed toward "Quality in Education." The quality of the teacher is the quality of the education. It is necessary to have the training; it is necessary to have the rewards that attract the superior people to the teaching profession; it is necessary to have the facilities, the plant, the resources, and all the rest that contribute to a strong program. Most of all we need the qualities of inspiration and dedication that make for great teaching.

As I have observed from my own experience, great teaching includes great love, sympathy and understanding of children, and recognition that children are individuals, not classes or groups. It calls for restraint and patience so that self-reliance may develop. Great teaching requires knowledge of and enthusiasm for the subject, and insistent projection across whatever resistances stand in the way. Great teaching succeeds in leading children out of themselves to consideration for their fellows, an awareness of the beauties of nature, a desire to read literature, and to acquire knowledge and put it to constructive use.

It is my observation, as a parent, that the goals of teaching are being realized in Minnesota today to a very great degree. That was evident to me when one of our youngsters came home from the first week of first grade. I asked him how he liked his new teacher, Miss Laura Schneider of St. Paul. "She's wonderful," was the reply. "She even loves the naughty ones." Just last week, another son and two of his pals drove to Willmar to visit their high school librarian at her summer cottage. These teachers are reaching their students, and giving of themselves in an admirable way. I hope that from your days here on beautiful Lake Koronis, you will return to your jobs this fall with new inspiration, new information and a spirit of dedication that you can communicate to all of the teachers who will be looking to you for leadership in the year ahead.

—August 13, 1959

PRESERVING SOCIETY: SUPPORTING PUBLIC SCHOOLS

Many a Minnesota elected official in the 1950s played a role in the dedication of a new school building. It was a fairly frequent event. As the baby boom generation reached school age and post-war suburban development exploded, the need for additional school facilities was pressing. School districts came to the voters time and again seeking approval for bond issues for school construction.

I was pleased to be invited to speak at the dedication of a new grade school in Falcon Heights in 1952. It was one of the finest facilities of its kind. The school district that built it, the Roseville district, had been created five years earlier, the first to be established under provisions of a 1947 school reorganization law. I much admired its progressive superintendent, Emmet Williams. He was so skillful at presenting the district's needs to the voters that he never lost a bond issue vote. Once he had a bond issue to build an addition on a building that was still under construction. Enrollment was mushrooming so rapidly that they had to build an addition before the school was even occupied. James Bryant Conant of Harvard University visited that Roseville School District, and in his book singled it out for praise as one of the best-conceived districts and programs that he had observed.

I'm convinced that Minnesota schools would still come in for favorable reviews, should a similar authority visit them today. But, regrettably, support for public education is not what it was a half-century ago. Bond issues don't win easy approval. Referenda to raise property taxes for school operations fail about as often as they succeed. The 2001 legislature committed the state to fund basic education costs, then promptly reneged on that promise. There has been so much emphasis on individuals making and accumulating money, and having low-cost government and reducing taxes. The whole philosophy has changed from the days when government was thought of as the instrument to realize the hopes of the people. There was an understanding that through taxation, a little coming from each person, mighty things could be done. There was an enthusiasm for bond issues and tax levies, as the means to a positive end.

Some people contend today that the quality of public education has deteriorated, and offer that excuse for withholding their support. My observation is that the quality of education is excellent for those who come prepared to learn. The problem has been not the quality of the education, but the condition of the students. Some of them come hungry. Some of them come addicted. Some of them come without much family unity or support. They have less chance to make the most of a learning opportunity. The best students today are far better educated than those of the past. Today's teaching is excellent. When people are fully prepared and of a mind to learn, the achievement possible today is greater than it ever was.

I suggested in 1952 that the first half of the twentieth century was not a good period for public education. It would be shameful if the same were said fifty years from now about our present time. Minnesota needs to guard against allowing an eagerness for accumulation of personal wealth to result in the sacrifice of our youth. If that happens, our future is at risk. Here is some of what I said at the Falcon Heights elementary school dedication:

⏭ It was in 1784 that the citizens of a small community in Massachusetts decided that they would like to name their town after Benjamin Franklin. They wrote to ask his consent to call their village Franklin, Massachusetts, and to suggest that he might wish to contribute a town bell as a token of his esteem. The response of Benjamin Franklin was interesting. He said that "sense being preferable to sound," he would send sixty-eight books as a foundation for a library, books "such as are most proper to inculcate the principles of sound religion and just governments."

This might have been just another example of the many practical good deeds of Benjamin Franklin, except for a coincidence of fate. In 1796, in Franklin, Massachusetts, Horace Mann was born. His education was very sketchy: the best of it centered in the local library that Franklin had established.

You may remember that Horace Mann, in 1837, facing a promising career in other fields, abandoned it all to become the first Secretary of the State Board of Education of Massachusetts. He was imbued with an almost fanatic belief in the importance of public school education. His work in arousing and inspiring teachers with a sense of the opportunities before them for accomplishing great and enduring work, made a tremendous contribution to the development of public school education. He is given the major credit for the revival of interest in public schools in New England and in the rest of the country.

His life and career are a mountaintop vantage point from which to look back toward still earlier history and forward to our own time.

One of the most significant developments affecting our country, and particularly we out in this part of the country, came about as the Articles of Confederation were up for ratification. When the thirteen Americas colonies won their independence from England, six of the old states, on the basis of their sea-to-sea grants, claimed sections of the great unsettled regions between the Allegheny Mountains and the Mississippi River. Maryland, having no such vast holdings, refused to ratify until the other states had given their western lands to the federal government for development in the interest of the entire country rather than for the few states that originally held them. The position of Maryland prevailed. Having acquired this vast territory, Congress had to devise a means of governing it. In 1787 an ordinance was passed, laying down the rates and regulations by which this area should be handled. This famous document, the Ordinance of 1787, is exceeded in importance only by the Constitution and Declaration of Independence, and is largely overlooked in some of our study of early

American history. It provided for the establishing of states in the new territory, allowed freedom of religion, habeas corpus, jury trial, and it also included the Jefferson provision originated in 1785 providing for survey and sale of land and for giving one thirty-sixth of the national domain to the new states for support of public schools. It declared, "Schools and the means of education shall forever be encouraged."

Although our pioneer statesmen felt deeply that the success of free government depended upon universal education, it is not mentioned in the Declaration of Independence, the Articles of Confederation or the United States Constitution. Many of the freedoms mentioned and made secure in these great documents are part of our Anglo-Saxon heritage, centuries in the making. Free and universal education is a unique contribution of our American people to the progress of mankind.

Horace Mann appeared just as our country was ready for a surge in interest in public school education. Under his direction, education in Massachusetts rose to the forefront, establishing the first normal school and a host of other firsts. Leaders in other states took up the work, and good progress was made. Here in our own territory and state, we were blessed with the vision of men like Alexander Ramsey, who proclaimed the education of the children as a primary responsibility of a free society that was to endure.

It should be remembered that progress has never been easy and never been without resistance. As recently as 1850 for example, in New York State, forty-two out of fifty-nine counties favored repeal of the law providing for free schools. There was widespread use of the argument that state monopoly, state despotism and state socialism would come if public schools became universal. There were many who felt that education for all was a waste of money. They were willing to recognize the necessity of certain professions needing education, but not the average citizen. Likewise, the education of girls and women lagged.

On the other hand, several factors encouraged the development of public education in the nineteenth century. Thousands of immigrants were coming here, and the parents were in no position to teach the children even the language of the new land. It was clear that if the United States was to develop as a nation, all-inclusive public education was essential. Another stimulus was the Industrial Revolution, which made reading, writing and figuring an important part of making a living. The working classes demanded tax-supported education. Still another factor was the rapid development of education in Europe, particularly in the German states after the Napoleonic Wars, which set an example for us.

It is possible that future historians will refer to the first half of the twentieth century as a low point in public school education, followed by a vigorous revival of interest. The First World War was a dislocating factor, and the Depression brought our school program to a low point from which we have not yet recovered. Financial support dwindled, physical plant deteriorated, teaching personnel declined, and until recent years the situation was very discouraging. You know what we have gone through in our own state, with teachers' strikes, closed schools, part-time classes, terrible overcrowding, and all of the other factors of an unsatisfactory situation.

Now, however, throughout the land, events similar to this one today are being held. New schools are being built. They are following designs unrestricted by tradition and adapted to the needs of today. Citizens are going to the polls and voting for the funds necessary to provide the plant, to hire the teachers, and to do the job that needs to be done. The current interest in improving our educational system is the strongest evidence that our vigorous society, in accordance with our traditional goals, will be preserved.

It is clear that we wish as many of our citizens as possible to lead fruitful and satisfying lives. We realize that in order to prosper as a highly industrialized nation, we must find and educate all varieties of talent and guide that talent into proper channels of employment. As Dr. Conant of Harvard and others have pointed out, we are going to live in a closely connected, highly industrialized world, which contains a vast amount of specialized knowledge. It is important that our horizons be broadened, that we become wiser and more stable individuals, less susceptible to the calls of modern medicine-men. The high degree of fluidity that has characterized our society must be preserved. We must maintain the American tradition that regardless of the circumstances into which a child may be born, there is no station in life to which that child may not aspire.

From the long view, it is probable that our unique contribution as a nation will not be in the field of abstract thought, art, or poetry. It may not be in our development and mass production of highly complicated mechanical instruments. Our enduring contribution is rather in a demonstration that a certain type of society, long dreamed of by idealists, can be closely approached in reality. That is, a free society in which the hopes and aspirations of a large part of the members can find enduring satisfaction through outlets once reserved for only a small minority of mankind.

In meeting this continuing challenge we must constantly adjust to the world in which we live. No one will deny that world peace is the paramount goal today. In our family life, our church life and our school life, there is the great need for a continuing emphasis on American idealism. Developing good character is our most important task. America has a destiny of world leadership that will require the fullest moral as well as mental and physical development of our most promising individuals.

The job is never ended, but today we share a great privilege. Today we are seeing one of the finest flowers of citizen effort—this splendid new facility, manned by competent instructors, led by men of vision, supported by a forward-looking citizenry. It is democracy at its best, and it contributes to our best hopes for a peaceful world.

—November 16, 1952

HIGHER EDUCATION

Higher education has always been of keen interest to me, in part because I experienced its value in my own life. If I had not had the opportunity to go to junior college in Muskegon, Michigan, at no cost the year after I graduated from high school, my life would have been very different. Had I not enrolled in the University of Minnesota a year after moving to this state, I likely would not have met my dear wife Eleanor, or acquired the skills and the confidence I needed to own a business, run for elective office, and contribute to community life. I could not have attended the university, were it not for its low tuition in those years.

I have long been concerned about the large number of bright high school students who do not go on to college. As a weekly newspaper publisher, I liked to keep in touch with some of the high school students in the communities our newspapers served. It grieved me how many students—bright, promising young people—would end their formal education when they completed high school. Some families seemed to think that college was a luxury activity for other people, or that the role of a high school graduating woman was to get married and have children, and the goal of a man was to get a job. Little consideration was given to the fact that much better jobs could be had if those young people had more education.

Until every child who can benefit from an education gets to college, we are lacking as a society. The time has come to make four years of college a public expense. A college degree is as much a necessity in today's economy as a high school education was when Horace Mann led his crusade to make high school education free. We are seeing evidence that rising tuition costs are keeping low-income students away from college, even as total enrollment has been rising. That trend will only serve to widen the gap between rich and poor in our society, as only those who already have means receive the education that will result in higher incomes. Some people are going to have wealth in perpetuity, while others never achieve it. That kind of stratification poses a danger to democracy. Every citizen in a democracy ought to have reason to believe that no matter where he was born, or with what means, he can aspire to the highest position.

Here is some of what I said about higher education at Mankato State College in 1959, on the occasion of the dedication of a building to my state Senate colleague, Val Imm:

⏭ Minnesota has always maintained great regard for the value of education. In his very first inaugural address to the territorial assembly in 1849, Alexander Ramsey called for generous support for the schools. Even before Minnesota became a state, the University of Minnesota was established. Following soon, the great structure of our overall education program was laid; the teachers colleges, now our state colleges, were founded; and steady and constant support through the years has maintained progress.

It would be wonderful if we could relax and view this record of accomplishment with complacency. The fact of the matter, of course, is that the people of our state face a challenge of very great proportions in the years ahead. Large numbers of pupils are filling our elementary and secondary schools, new buildings are being built, new demands are being made. Though rapid has been the growth of our colleges, they are yet to feel the full impact of the wartime increase in birth rate. Questions of curriculum command attention, problems of organization and administration are before us, as is the very real fact of revenue needs.

Serious questions are being raised by weary taxpayers about the cost of education. Some are asking, Can we afford such fine colleges and a university? If we will but stop for a moment to consider the matter, we will realize there can be but one answer: Yes, we can afford them. Even more emphatically: We certainly cannot afford to neglect higher education.

Sometimes it is said that there are some students attending college who should not be there. I believe there is greater truth in the statement, however, that there are a great many young people who should be in college who are not there. A survey reported in the October 1958 issue of *Science Magazine* disclosed that Minnesota was fourth among all the states in the number of near-winners in the 1957 National Merit Scholarship competition. The sad part of the story is that Minnesota ranked forty-second—almost at the bottom—in the number of those near-winners who went on to college. Eighty-four percent of those who failed to go to college indicated that financial limitations kept them from continuing their education. To lose this resource of superior ability is tragic in the present situation of world affairs. To discharge the role of leadership that is ours, we need all the talent we can muster.

That great prophet of our republic, de Tocqueville, said in 1830 that the crucial test for American democracy would be in the development of the superior individual. We need to improve our techniques for identifying the superior individual, we need to improve our programs in elementary and secondary schools for developing the full potential of the superior individual, and it is of the greatest importance for us to make sure that resources and facilities are available to develop that talent to its fullest degree in colleges and universities.

A large number of this class are going into the field of education. Yours is a tremendous challenge and a very great opportunity to work with the children who will come under your influence, to further develop your own abilities to identify the superior individual, and then to lend the weight of your interest and influence toward directing those children to colleges that will develop their full abilities.

Today as I drove to Mankato, I thought to myself, as I have so many times before, what a host of benefits are ours to enjoy. We have material comforts that were undreamed of but a few years ago, we drive on highways that could be hardly imagined by our parents and grandparents. Just two years ago, when I heard a speaker tell about the proposed launching of a satellite during the geophysical year, I looked around at the other people in the room to see if any of the others thought that he was joking. Surely he could not be serious. Yet, as we talk, satellites are orbiting around the Sun.

With all the progress that has been made, surely we will not fall short of the responsibilities that we face in the future. Expenditures must be scrutinized carefully, tax programs must be developed with the greatest concern for equitability, needs in many areas deserve consideration. But we must pledge ourselves to maintain our faith in educating every individual, for it is that which has created the great success of our country.

—March 6, 1959

PREPARING YOUNG PEOPLE FOR CITIZENSHIP

Life, to me, is fairly serious. It isn't a joy ride. There are responsibilities to family, to country, and to personal identity that should be fulfilled. An understanding of those responsibilities ought to be instilled in young people, as part of their education to be citizens of a democracy.

Not all of that education happens in the classroom. Extra-curricular activities such as debate and athletics can teach a great deal. When young people work together as a team, they learn to get along with others and cooperate in achieving a mutual goal. Knowing how to do that is crucial to the effectiveness not only of the individual, but also of society.

I very strongly feel that a great need exists to teach individuals to speak well in public. Much misunderstanding comes about because people of limited vocabulary or limited ability of self-expression are unable to convey their thoughts.

They are handicapped in their capacity to contribute to public debate. American schools today place great emphasis on athletics. While that kind of team activity has merit, it should not eclipse other extra-curricular activities, especially those involving public speaking. Debate, I think, is of the greatest importance. To learn to think clearly and speak persuasively is a great asset, no matter what career a person follows.

New technology has given new, fascinating toys to young people, and those things too are overemphasized. Computer and video games and a steady diet of spectator sports and entertainment on television consume a great deal of young people's time, in ways that are not really productive or expansive of the human personality. Those things are passive. They involve being entertained, rather than doing and participating and being challenged. Watching TV, you can almost feel yourself being submerged in sound and fury. The programming is often purposely directed to the lowest common denominator of understanding, so people of ability are held back rather than encouraged. Adults should guide young people away from consuming excessive amounts of time in front of television and computer screens.

We were decades away from video and computer games in 1962, when as governor I spoke to the annual Merit Reception for contributors to programming at Coffman Memorial Union at the University of Minnesota. Yet what I said then about activities that prepare young people for citizenship has abiding relevance. Here is an excerpt from that address:

⏭ Extra-curricular activities are vital to the total development of the individual. In his academic pursuits, the student is on the receiving end: he listens to someone lecture or he reads a textbook. It is through extra-curricular activities that he is stimulated to personal participation, to have ideas of his own—some of which are good, some a little wild. Communicating ideas generates experience, which is fundamental to the development of a useful citizen.

The greatest single need in the area of citizenship in our state and in our country is participation. I do not believe our greatest enemy is Communism, the Birch Society or the other ultra-isms of one kind or another. The greatest danger is indifference, the kind where the people do not know or do not care what is going on. It is frustrating for a legislative body or a governor's office when many people do not care. Personal involvement is vital to our continuation as a country.

Almost every day there are groups of students touring the Capitol, and I usually interrupt just about anything I am doing to go out and visit with them a few minutes. I generally try to bring out very quickly the three branches of government and their duties. Then I ask, "Who do you think in our state and federal governments is the most important?" Frequently they will say, the president; and I will reply, "He is important, but not most important." Then they will mention the governor, Congress, or the Supreme Court, and I will always bring out how important these people are, but that they are not most important. Then someone usually comes up with the idea of the people; and, of course, this is the answer. This is the unique quality that makes our country great—the people are the government. This does not mean just the mass of people, it means people as individuals—people who are alert and informed, who also participate. You cannot escape the responsibilities of citizenship.

Some people say they will not get involved. One cannot help but be involved. One of the best examples of this is the way we amend our state constitution. As you know the legislature proposes the amendment, submits it to the people, and they vote on it. If the majority of the people voting in the election vote for the amendment, it carries. The people that go into the polls look at all the fine print and say: "Oh my, I do not know anything about it, I do not think I will vote." These people are still voting, because their vote counts "no." For an amendment to pass, there must be a majority vote of everyone who votes in the election. Their indifference is registered as a "no" vote. The fact that they are citizens and are voting requires that they become informed and participate. This, I think, is one of the great values of participation in extra-curricular activities: It stimulates an awareness of individual responsibility.

I am sure that most of the students who come to the university are a little overwhelmed by its size and the large number of students. They probably have a feeling of insignificance, ineffectiveness and futility, and consider themselves just one little person in a great big crowd. But then some of the students begin to feel that there are some opportunities, and some things that need to be done. These students feel the need to participate. There is a satisfaction in doing a job—any kind of a job—and filling a need.

As you begin to participate, an amazing thing happens. You begin to realize that one person can make a whale of a difference. Most of the great things that have been accomplished in history have been accomplished by some one person who had the dedication and commitment to do something. I once had a wonderful luncheon visit with Dr. Donald Cowling, former president of Carleton. He was discussing what makes a person great. We talked about great ability, and quickly had to discard that idea. Ability is no measure of greatness, because there are some very intelligent crooks. We arrived at (and I am sure he was guiding my thinking) a definition of greatness: the degree of commitment to a great idea. Commitment is an individual experience—the experience you get through participation.

At our house we enjoy reading, and we like to study Minnesota history. One thing that constantly impresses me is a certain characteristic of early Minnesota explorers. They not only participated, but they had some sense of significance, a feeling that they—each person—could make a difference. This is one of the great benefits of extra-curricular activities. You discover that if you want to, you can influence meetings and decisions. You can have an influence. This, I think, is the great need in our modern life from the standpoint of government and citizenship—the need to understand that each individual makes a difference. We are individual, so different, that every person has some contribution to make. The amazing thing is that if you have an opportunity to contribute and do not, no one else can make just the contribution that you could have made because there is not anybody else like you—there never has and never will be. The earlier the individual begins to develop a sense of responsibility, a desire to participate and a desire to achieve, the better off we will be.

—May 15, 1962

HAMLINE UNIVERSITY

I never cease to be amazed at the courage, vision and sacrifice of the early settlers in Minnesota. It is incredible to think of a little town of 300 people—a majority of them unschooled native Americans—having the courage to establish a university. That is what the people of Red Wing and the Methodist Church did in 1854. To do it, and then to endure the vagaries of depressions and wars that interfered with progress, and still carry it forward to thrive to this day, is a marvelous record of achievement. That is the story of Hamline University, Minnesota's oldest college. I recounted that story for a Hamline audience in 1979.

Minnesota's private liberal arts colleges are some of this state's most prized assets. I consider them essential to our way of life. They are havens of culture. They provide their students and their communities with valuable exposure to literature, science, languages, history, the ideas and the arts of the world. They broaden Minnesota's horizons. I constantly tell young people, "Don't be too quick to pick your specialty. Take four years of liberal arts training and get a view of life and a view of the world. Then, in the process, you'll meet instructors or you'll be inspired or you'll get ideas as to your own ability, and you'll find the field in which you should major. Then, after liberal arts college, go to the specialty."

The legislature has recognized the value of a private liberal arts education by designing the state-funded student aid program so that needy Minnesota students at private colleges can receive state grants. Grants are available to students accepted at an accredited college in the state, either public or private. It's just like giving people a loan to buy a car, and allowing them to choose any car they desire. That program has been criticized for allowing too much public money to flow to private institutions. But I consider it a wise investment, both in young lives and in colleges and universities that are of great benefit to Minnesota.

Here is some of what I said about Hamline, on the occasion of its 125th birthday celebration:

⏭ By 1849, when Minnesota became a territory, there were a few small village schools, opened by missionaries of the various denominations for the instruction in reading and writing of such Indians as took readily to these refinements of Christian civilization; but there was as yet no provision for what we would now call secondary education and certainly not collegiate education. The need of a higher grade of schools soon made itself felt. The Methodist Church was the first to move in the matter.

As early as 1850 there began to be talk of organizing an academy or seminary, but before any decided action had been taken the project had grown to the dimensions of a university. Application for a charter was made, and in 1854, a charter for a university was granted by the legislature, and Bishop Leonidas Hamline gave an endowment of $25,000, providing the new institution a financial base. The school was incorporated under the name of the Trustees of the Hamline University of Minnesota, this name being adopted in honor of its founder and to distinguish it from other institutions which might receive the name of Bishop Hamline, who had given at the same time a like amount to endow a college in Iowa.

The legislature, being eager to have educational institutions established in the territory, was disposed to grant a liberal charter. It fixed the location of the institution on the Mississippi River between

St. Paul and Lake Pepin. Red Wing, then a struggling river town with a sparsely settled country back of it, was selected as the site. In 1849 Red Wing's Village, as it was then called, had a population of 305, the 300 being Sioux Indians, and the five being two missionaries, the wife and child of one of them, and a farmer. The Indians lived in bark huts scattered over a small portion of the present city. Pursuant to the terms of a treaty, when the grass grew in the spring of 1853, the Indians vacated the town. The non-Indian inhabitants then numbered twenty. In November of the following year, Hamline was opened for academic work, with only one or two teachers and an attendance of probably about sixty preparatory [high school] students.

In 1857 the university proper was opened, being the first and for some years thereafter the only collegiate institution in Minnesota. One might ask, don't I recall that the University of Minnesota was established by the first territorial assembly in 1849?

The answer would be yes, but that in its earliest years the University of Minnesota was also a preparatory school, not a college-level institution. In fact, it went into dormancy for a period of years, just as Hamline did, as we shall see, and the University of Minnesota as an institution of higher education came into being in 1869 when it was brought back to life and William Watts Folwell was called to become its president.

Besides being the first college organized in Minnesota, Hamline University enjoys the distinction of being among the first colleges of the United States to establish a scientific course of equal rank with a classical, and in affording to young women the same educational facilities as to young men. The latter was a daringly novel idea at the time, the thought that men and women should be educated in the same schools and by the pursuit of the same studies. In 1859 there were two candidates for the degree of Bachelor of Arts and both were women. The class of the following year also consisted of two women. From that time until the University closed in 1869, more women than men were recommended for graduation.

It was the business depression of 1857 and the War Between the States that were the undoing of Hamline University at Red Wing, plus a growing desire on the part of some to relocate in the capital city. When the Red Wing campus was closed in 1869, the city bought the property for enough money to permit the college to pay off its debts and leave free of obligation.

It had been the intention to re-establish the university in St. Paul within a few years, but in 1873 another financial depression hit and, although a suitable tract of land had been found in St. Paul, at the present location, it was several years before the re-opening. In 1880, Minnesota was entering upon an era of prosperity and commercial progress, and the time was ripe for Hamline University to reopen.

A building was built, known as University Hall, which stood almost alone on the prairie between the two cities of St. Paul and Minneapolis. It contained all the recitation rooms used by the college, the chapel, library, dormitories and boarding department. Two years later, a boarding hall was built for the accommodation of young women. It was completed just as a fresh misfortune befell the institution, the burning of the original building. Probably the greatest loss was all of the records that existed at that time. This tragedy constitutes a continuing barrier to obtaining the details of some of the early St. Paul and Red Wing history.

University Hall was immediately rebuilt, and other buildings were added. The dedication of the new University Hall marked the beginning of the administration of Reverend George H. Bridgeman, who was elected in 1883 and served until 1912. His administration was one of enormous growth and development for Hamline.

Hamline has many firsts to its credit. While still at Red Wing, it established the first law school in the state of Minnesota, graduating two classes before dropping law from the curriculum in 1863. Similarly, Hamline had one of the very early medical departments in our state, established in 1895 when Hamline took over the Minneapolis College of Physicians and Surgeons. The medical school was located in Minneapolis, it had its own faculty and recommended candidates to the Hamline Board of Trustees for medical degrees. It conferred 300 M.D. degrees before it was merged with the medical school of the University of Minnesota in 1908.

Surely the occasion of a 125th Anniversary is a time to salute any institution durable enough to survive for that length of time.

Yet from some standpoints, 125 years is a relatively short period in which to accomplish so much. Not too many years ago I was serving in the state Senate with Ole Sageng, an elderly man who could recall hearing a speech of Governor Samuel A. Van Sant in 1901. Alexander Ramsey, the first territorial governor of Minnesota, was seated on the stage. It brought home to me that the history of Minnesota is encompassed in two lifetimes.

When one tries to envision barren Red Wing in 1854, one becomes totally amazed at the courage and vision of those pioneers who persevered through every sort of difficulty to keep this institution alive, and get it on a solid road to progress. Hamline has come through all the trials and tribulations of its first 125 years with strength and quality, and is ready to take long strides into the future.

—October 4, 1979

WHAT IS A LIBRARY?

A library is a community's temple of learning. It was my joy to assist Princeton, Minnesota, in the construction of a new library in the early 1990s. It was a major project for the town of 4,000 people, one vigorously supported by the local newspaper, the *Princeton Union-Eagle*. That newspaper is the flagship of ECM Publishing, a company I founded and, in those years, headed. Today its chief executive is our son Julian.

I tried to stretch the imagination of the people of Princeton about the nature of the project. Some townspeople thought a remodeled old building would do for a new library. I disagreed: "If you needed a new church, you wouldn't look around for some old building to remodel. You'd build a new building, as a symbol of your faith. Well, a library is a symbol of culture, a symbol of literary achievement, of the finest ideas that have ever occurred to humanity. It's worthy of a new building." That argument prevailed, though it took some doing over a period of years to live up to our budget in excess of $1 million.

We need to speak up for libraries again today. State and local government budgets are falling short, and library funding is being cut. That should not happen. Library needs should be met. If that means higher taxes, well, I'm reminded of the old movie short advertising a program by Olson and Johnson, great comedians of an earlier time. It told how wonderful the show would be, and added at the end, "There will be a slight formality at the box office." I think we should think of taxes as a slight formality. We get so much for what we pay. People are misled when they are told that they will be better off if services are cut. Services like libraries are the backbone of the community. They are worth whatever they cost.

At the library's dedication, I paid tribute to a great governor who had died two days before, Governor Rudy Perpich. His memory will live in history as one who aspired for much, and accomplished much. The Mall of America, the National Sports Center in Blaine, the new Minnesota Historical Society building, and the World Trade Center in St. Paul are only a few of the things he championed. He was one who stood for investing in amenities, and joining hands to attempt great things together. He wouldn't be demanding "no new taxes" today. He would be calling for no closure of libraries.

Here is some of what I said at the Princeton library dedication:

⏭ What is a library? At the high school now, they call the library the media center. I don't like that word much because it has such a cold, technological ring to it. To me, really, a library is more an attitude of mind, a set of values that can be reflected in many ways.

What do you dedicate a library to? First, we'd mention dedication to children. It is a satisfaction to see children all over the place, looking at books, loving books. Last night, I read Longfellow's poem about the story hour. I think if every parent of young children was required to read that poem about the children who climbed up on grandfather's lap while he read to them, and the joy they felt, they'd want to have something like that going on.

We'd want to dedicate the library to the love of learning. There is a love of learning that sometimes gets lost. Young children are so eager for information. Parents can be driven wild with youngsters who keep saying, "Why? Why?" It's wonderful to have that desire to know. The inquiring mind of a child is a blessing that people can retain as long as they live.

Another dedication could be to lifetime learning. Today, to go to school, go to college, get training, get degrees, and stop there? That's fatal economically. There's so much new information being generated that unless people are constantly renewing themselves, they become obsolete. As a judge once told a lawyer who had been practicing for a long time, "You know, all the laws you know have been repealed and replaced."

Along with these go freedom of expression. There you get into an area that has been a controversy in society for hundreds of years. John Milton, who ranks with Shakespeare as one of the greatest literary figures, wrote one of the finest appeals to the English government to not censure literature. I once talked with one of the executives of the university about some of the rules and regulations of the American Association of University Professors that can get in the way of the freedom and initiative you like to have. He said, "Elmer, there are abuses and it is bad, but the alternative is so much worse." It's the same thing that was characterized by Churchill when he talked about democracy: that it's the worst government in the world, except all the others. Freedom of expression can be abused and sometimes can be irritating. It can sometimes be downright offensive, but the alternative is so much worse. When you lose freedom, you lose the essence of life itself. Freedom! Freedom is a dedicatory word that should hang in every library.

It's a wonderful day. It's a wonderful opportunity, and the beginning to setting a standard for what we in Princeton can really do in the way of public enterprise. One thing we tried to inculcate in ourselves is that we should never ask the price first. We should always ask, "What should we be doing? What should we aspire to?"

Minnesota lost a great leader this week who was known for his vision, former Governor Rudy Perpich. He had more ideas than one could ever hope to accomplish. Many of them didn't work out very well, but many of them did. He forever wanted the best for Minnesota, for Minnesota to be in the center of the world because it was in the center of the North American continent, neatly halfway between Asia and Europe. We do well to remember him and his vision today.

This library can set a standard. There can be the finest life that anybody ever had in all the history of this world right here in Princeton, partly by what's here, partly by what we can now reach through an information network all over the world. This is an incredible time to be alive.

—September 23, 1995

BOTANICAL BOOKS

Eleanor and I have had a special attachment to the University of Minnesota Landscape Arboretum since its founding in the late 1950s. It brought together several of our interests in a remarkable way. We were both lovers of nature. We had a dear friendship with Leon Snyder, the head of the university's horticulture department and of the arboretum, and his wife Vera. They were tireless workers on the arboretum's behalf.

Then there was our love of books, and our idea that the arboretum might include a horticultural library. I loved seeking out books that would contribute to such a library. Through years of studying and collecting books, I came to know about herbals and botanicals—beautiful catalogs of flowers and plants, prepared and published in the seventeenth and eighteenth centuries and prized for medical as well as horticultural purposes. The characters involved in these books are tremendous. Carolus Linnaeus, for example, undertook single-handedly to change the method of describing plants and animals. He invented the Linnaeus system of description that is used to this day. One copy of an herbal book contained an amusing portrait of Linnaeus dressed as a Laplander.

Nicholas Culpeper, who compiled *Culpeper's Complete Herbal*, was also an astrologer. He believed that herbs had to be harvested at a certain time in order to yield their full benefits. Sometimes, this was at night under certain signs of the stars. He claimed to be able to cure every illness known to man. Reading his herbal is a treat because it mixes astrology, medicine, superstition and all manner of fun things.

Perhaps the most noteworthy herbal artist was Pierre-Joseph Redouté, who made drawings of roses and lilies that are unsurpassed in beauty. Redouté was the official painter for the Empress Josephine, the wife of Napoleon, and enjoyed the patronage of a number of luminaries in French society in the late eighteenth and early nineteenth centuries. I was fortunate to begin collecting rare books for the arboretum in the 1960s, when prices were low. We were so pleased to get at auction a set of Redouté prints in both color and black and white that is one of only eight copies in existence. Today, it is almost beyond price.

I love sharing things we have learned and the joy we have derived from our involvement with the arboretum's Andersen Horticultural Library. This excerpt is from the Kermit A. Olson memorial lecture at the University of Minnesota's Department of Horticulture:

⏭ Printing as a tool of mankind is relatively modern when compared to botany. From the earliest times man depended upon his knowledge of plants for food, shelter, clothing and medicines.

As man struggled for understanding, knowledge and wisdom he invented powers, natural and supernatural. It was in the glory days of Greece that the challenge of demonstrable truth began to modify the paradigm of the age.

One of the most significant students of Aristotle was Theophrastus. He was bequeathed the manuscripts and library of Aristotle and was made the guardian of Aristotle's children. Theophrastus wrote two important botanical treatises, *On The History Of Plants* in nine books and *On The Causes of Plants* in six books. These works are considered the most important contributions to botanical science during antiquity and the Middle Ages. Theophrastus was the leader of the Peripatetic school for thirty-five years; he died in 287 B.C. He is acclaimed as the "father of botany" and his work dominated the scene for eighteen centuries.

Just as influential for nearly as long was Dioscorides, the Greek medical man who raised medical botany to the level of an applied science. In *Materia Medica* he described the properties and uses of more than 500 medicinal plants. That work was the supreme authority in its field for centuries.

By the end of the fifteenth century, printing presses were being established throughout Europe and the demands for books were insatiable. Among the earliest books printed were two from manuscripts that had been available for a long time. One, *Liber de Proprietatibus Rerum* by Bartholomaeus Anglicus, a monk, was printed about 1470 and reprinted twenty-five times by 1500. It was an alphabetical arrangement of a large number of trees and herbs, with emphasis on medicinal properties. The second was the *Book of Nature* by Konrad printed at Augsburg in 1475 by Hanns Bamler, listing Latin and German names of herbs, vegetables, shrubs and trees with description and attributes. Another printing of an early manuscript was the *Herbarium* of Apuleius Platonicus. It is believed to have been compiled in the fifth or sixth century, and thus traveled by manuscript for about a thousand years before its first printing.

Soon after, three important works were printed in Mainz, Germany, *Latin Herbarius* (1484) *German Herbarius* (1485), and in 1491 the *Hortus* or *Ortus Sanitatis.* In the early sisteenth century, Germany contributed significantly with the work of Brunfels, Fuchs, Bock and Cordus. Bock was an accurate observer, and his great work was the *New Kreutter Buch* printed in 1539. Considered the masterpiece of herbal scholarship was Fuchs' Latin *De Historia Stirpium* printed in Switzerland in 1542. It dealt with about one hundred foreign plants, and five hundred native German species. Commenting on his work, Fuchs said "there is nothing pleasanter and more delightful than to wander over woods, mountains, plains, garlanded and adorned with flowerlets and plants of various sorts, and most elegant to boot, and to gaze intently upon them. But it increases that pleasure not a little, if there be added an acquaintance with the virtues and powers of these same plants."

Culpeper was a part of the seventeenth century's very unscientific astrological botany. He published *A Physicall Directory* in 1649 that was incredible in claims of efficacious treatment. Despite attacks by the medical establishment of the time, his writings went into many editions.

As a sample of his prescriptions, let me read what the berries of the juniper bush will do, from Culpeper's *Herbal* published in 1798: "This admirable solar shrub can scarcely be equaled for its virtues. Its berries are hot in the third degree, and dry in the first, being a excellent counter-poison and a great resister of pestilence; they are very good for the bites of venomous beasts. It is so powerful a remedy for the dropsy, that, by drinking only the lye made of the ashes of this herb, it cures the disease, helps the fits of the mother, strengthens the stomach and expels wind; indeed there are few better remedies for the wind and colic than the chemical oil drawn from the berries. They are also good for a cough, shortness of breath, consumption, pains in the belly, ruptures, cramps and convulsions; they strengthen the brain, help the memory, fortify the sight by strengthening the optic nerve and give safe and speedy delivery to women in labor. The ashes of the wood are a special remedy for the scurvy in the gums, by rubbing them therewith; the berries stay all fluxes, help the hemorrhoids or piles, and kill worms in children; they break the stone, procure lost appetite, and are very good for palsies and falling sickness. A lye made of the ashes of the wood, and the body bathed therewith, cures the itch, scabs and leprosy." I'm sure you are persuaded to go get some juniper bush berries!

It is a remarkable coincidence that the invention of printing came just as scientific botany was emerging and made it possible to record, illustrate and preserve the fascinating developments of the last four centuries. Our modern age has produced many new forms of communication and illustration, but there can be no question that the heritage of botanical printing will always have a special worth and appeal to the researcher, the student, and the lover of fine books.

—Feb. 11, 1987

FUNDING THE UNIVERSITY

I've had many wonderful experiences, but one of the choicest was when Senate Majority Leader Roger Moe called me in March 2001 and invited me to speak to the Minnesota Senate. I very much appreciated my years in the Senate, and have great respect for the body. I knew that it was very unusual to invite a former senator or anyone else to address the Senate. There were occasions when joint sessions were held for some international figure, but to be invited to speak to the Senate alone was a rare privilege that I eagerly accepted.

From the time I was invited until the time I started speaking, my thoughts were occupied with considering what I ought to say. I memorized a list of things I wanted to say. I learned by heart some of the budget figures, so that I could recite them accurately when I commented on the budget deliberations that were then in progress. I was super-charged when the time came. I greatly appreciated the arrangements that had been made to lift me a little higher than the floor of the Senate, so that I could have the effect of a podium while remaining seated in my wheelchair.

I poured out my heart to the Senate. I did not just reminisce. I wanted to make some timely points about one aspect of their budget debate. I urged them to generously fund the University of Minnesota. It is the most important institution in the state, and should command priority in any state budget. The governor then was Jesse Ventura, who was not as attuned to the university's importance as a governor ought to be. His budget request for the university was a disappointment, one I asked the Senate to correct. Here is some of what I said:

⏭ I'm so thrilled to be here, I'm like an old nag feeling like a racehorse. I know what a rare honor it is to be invited to speak to this body. I came to have a good time and I hope you did, too. I don't see very well and I don't hear very well and I don't move very well, but I can still talk. So, someday if you hear a disembodied voice around here, you can explain, "That's just old Elmer, still talking."

There are three experiences I've had lately that I'd like to share with you. One was seeing a TV documentary called *Liberty! The American Revolution*. It is a wonderful history of the events leading up to the Revolutionary War, the incredible sacrifice of people in the Revolutionary War and, then, the magnificent actions leading up to the formation of our constitutional government.

One of the most touching parts of the whole program are letters from Abigail Adams to her husband, John Adams, at the Continental Congress. She always had a salutation, "Dearest Friend." He would write back, "My Dearest Friend." She would write to him, "Don't forget the ladies." In one letter particularly, she kind of emphasized with a little harshness in her voice—though the letters were very tender—"Don't forget the ladies or they'll have to look out for themselves." At that early date, Abigail Adams was a feminist, bless her heart. Anyone who sees that documentary for six hours, well, if tears don't come to their eyes of gratitude for this country and what it means and what people did to bring it about, they would be hard-hearted indeed.

My friend Wy Spano was the lead author on a book called *Minnesota*. That would be an interesting handbook for every new legislator to receive, because it's a marvelous depiction of how Minnesota works, where it came from, and the wonderful job it has done as a state. I used to wonder when Athens realized what a great city it was. Maybe it didn't occur to the people who lived there at the time. We admire Athens after all these years as a city of culture, refinement, learning, and many other fine qualities. I wonder when people are going to *really* realize how wonderful Minnesota is, how closely it comes to achieving the balance of peace among people and prosperity for all. It's not perfect, and I'll get around to a couple of suggestions.

I've been so thankful that my father came to this country from Norway. I'm proud of my Norwegian heritage. I visited Norway and think highly of that little country, but there's nowhere near the opportunity there that there has been for me in Minnesota, to have the benefit of its education, to have the benefit of its public services. I constantly learn of new ones. As I've grown old, I've come to use some of the services you provide. You may not know how important they are to people. One, for example, is the single channel free radio that broadcasts twenty-four hours a day to people who are visually impaired. The other is a tape recorder/player that hooks you up to 150,000 books in the Library of Congress so that you can hear and read fine books, hear and read the news. I listen to *Newsweek* every week on tape. It's wonderful, the services that Minnesota provides.

As for the third experience: There's a new book by Ann Pflaum and some other authors of the history of the University of Minnesota since 1945. It is an historic record and the luminaries, the national and international figures, that have brought fame to our state, that have brought service to mankind, that have brought jobs to Minnesota, make a compelling story.

That brings me to question the budget. I don't know all about the budget at the university, but I believe that's one area where the good Governor [Jesse] Ventura is lacking in previous experience, and it shows. I meant to mention one point. I had a call the other day from the XFL saying that they were thinking of some changes in their personnel, and wondered if I'd be interested.

I've kept in touch with the medical school, and it's been sliding down. It doesn't rank nationally as high as it did twenty years ago. I know the need of the medical school right now. There is $16 million definitely needed to just balance the budget of clinical services. It used to be that clinical services brought income to the university, but under all the complications that exist today, they're running behind at the rate of about $8 million a year. They need $16 million just to pay the bills. It's absolutely essential they get that $16 million, and I believe it is in Governor Ventura's budget. But, there's also $10 million needed to beef up the faculty. There are surgeons there who would like to retire, but they can't in good conscience retire when the need is so great and personnel are so limited. It takes everybody's help to train doctors these days. There's so much to learn about new technology, new medicines, new procedures. Minnesota has been in the vanguard for many years in medical advances. Then, there's $1.2 million needed for medical technologists who are an important part of the health care system.

I think the best investment that could be made would be to give the university the tools to do their job. To cut them back to some minimum of 25 percent of the increase they asked for [as Ventura proposed] is hazardous to the state's welfare, and is certainly discounting the future. The university is the engine that drives the economy. It generates the jobs. It generates the research. It generates the students.

My life has been tremendously changed by the influence of the university. The best thing that happened to me there was I met my wife at the university, and it has meant so much. I would make a special plea for the university and for all of its needs. This is the time to invest in the future. I used to think and I still think and I still say to anybody who will listen, that in my view the dollars that people in our state have spent in taxes have brought them the best return of any money they've spent. I'm not a low tax person. There needs to be careful consideration of every investment made, but they should be ready to be made.

I have such tremendous respect for legislators. I have respect for the governor [Ventura]. He's brought a refreshing note, and he's had some good ideas. There is such a concern about tax cuts and rebates. Particularly with the volatile stock market and the changes that have taken place since budgets were put together last August, there's a new situation now, and there needs to be a reconsideration of rebates and tax cuts. The people of Minnesota would rather see their university restored and the needs of people met, rather than to have a rebate that slips away without having much of any impact. The secret of democracy is each contributing something. That way, the whole amounts to a great deal.

I think of this building, this chamber, this Capitol building. Think of it, less than fifty years after statehood, there was a need for a new state capitol. In 1895, a commission was appointed and some money appropriated to build a capitol. Instead of carrying it down to the minimum, instead of doing what they thought they could afford, they had a vision of what the state of Minnesota was going to be, and that it should have a capitol worthy of the state that was to be. They built this magnificent Capitol building, complete with a wonderful dome and gold horses and Italian marble all over the place. What a vision! What a challenge! What an inspiration! I can't help but think, wouldn't it be wonderful if 100 years from now it could be said, "That legislature of 2001 really did the job! They really had the vision. They made the investment."

What will people think a hundred years from now that you did? I challenge you, and I'd be so proud of you if you make the provision that is needed to put Minnesota in the forefront of the states. We've learned to live with being a high tax state and we've learned to enjoy the culture, all the amenities that that has brought. It means so much to people. I can vouch for that now, having lived so long and having passed through many stages.

I hope I haven't offended anyone. I'm so glad you came. I thank you from the bottom of my heart for this wonderful opportunity.

—March 19, 2001

V. WORLD CITIZENSHIP

THE UNITED NATIONS

The goal of creating a true world community seemed within humankind's grasp after both of the world wars of the twentieth century. It seems more elusive today. We have slipped in our progress toward world community, and to my sorrow, the United States has been a leader in the slippage. In fact, the United Nations has come to be regarded with some derision in the United States, and that's a terribly unfortunate thing.

The United States has let its UN dues become in default. We haven't paid our share of the expenses. We haven't filled a position that we're entitled to have in the United Nations, in UNESCO and the other agencies. We have not depended on the world organization, or fostered it. We encourage international agreements, but then, when the time comes to sign, we refuse to sign such basic ones as the non-proliferation of nuclear weapons. What is even worse, we unilaterally discard treaties we've made with other nations. We are so arrogant in our dealing with other nations that one wonders what the ultimate outcome will be. I fear that it may take the horror of a nuclear war for the United States to realize that there is no alternative to world community and world citizenship.

Americans need to recognize that we are diminished when all the world is criticizing our unilateral stance, just as we diminish others by denying them opportunities for a safer, more prosperous life that an effective world community would bring. An example of what is possible can be found in the work of Rotary International, of which I am a member. When

Sauk polio vaccine was discovered, it wasn't long before polio disappeared from the United States. Rotary undertook to make the world free of polio. It seemed to be an impossible mission at first, but for twenty years, they've been working away at it and have very nearly succeeded. In about another ten years, the whole world will be free of polio because of Rotary's united action.

I believe very strongly in the United Nations. I liken the necessity of risking some of our sovereignty through UN participation to the risk the thirteen original American states faced as they formed a new nation. The Articles of Confederation that were in force immediately after the Revolutionary War sought to maintain the independence of the thirteen states, and as a result, they did not work. Fortunately, the representatives who came together to solve the confederation's problems decided a new form of government was needed. Our constitution was the result, and centralized government became the rule. That was a big change for the people at the time, just as it's a big change now to think in world terms. But it's absolutely vital, and the sooner we get to it, the better.

Industry has a wonderful opportunity to show leadership and use its muscle to bring the United States into close alliance with the world community. It's no secret that recently, government in the United States has been weighted very strongly in favor of big business. Businesses know the economic importance of international cooperation. They also know that multi-national enterprises can operate successfully. Many corporations now operate on a worldwide basis. They have plants in all nations, and they operate in all markets. They are showing that it can be done—that cooperation works.

Do Americans have to have the entire world criticizing us? Do we have to have the entire world diminished because of us, when the opportunities are so great? I think Americans are ready to seize those opportunities, and are waiting for their leaders to show the way.

I spoke several times during the late 1960s, while the Vietnam War escalated, on the importance of the United Nations. What follows are excerpts from three such speeches. The first is taken from remarks on the occasion of the first flying of a United Nations flag over the Minneapolis City Hall:

⏭ I am deeply honored and tremendously thrilled to be a member of this distinguished company on this occasion. Not only does this occasion mark the first flying of the United Nations flag by Minneapolis and Hennepin County, but the first such declaration and UN flag flying by any major community in the United States. Thus this becomes a deeply significant occasion in our nation's history. It represents a commitment to cooperation among nations for world peace, to belief in the common brotherhood of all men of all nations, and to aspirations for a world community of peace, freedom and justice under world law.

If one thinks in terms of narrow nationalism, it is perfectly clear that one nation can have objectives that are in opposition to another nation, and that lacking any other influence, differences can grow into disputes and disputes into war. It can become a patriotic purpose for the men of one nation to seek to kill the men of another nation. On the other hand, if people believe that all men are bound together in a common humanity and that the dignity of any man is greater than the difference created by man-made boundaries, it becomes difficult, if not impossible, to wage war anywhere. It becomes as horrendous to kill anyone as one's own brother, for indeed, all men become brothers.

What is developing today is an ever-increasing body of opinion that holds that we must look upon all the peoples of the world as one community, and we must find a way to operate under a body of world law to preserve peace. Is the idea of a world community completely impractical?

Trygve Lie [first secretary general of the United Nations] didn't think so. In 1950, his tenth point in a twenty-year program for achieving peace through the United Nations read: "Active and systematic use of all the powers of the Charter and all the machinery of the United Nations to speed up the development of international law, towards an eventual enforceable world law for a universal world society."

Dag Hammarskjold [another U.N. secretary-general] said, "The dilemma of our age, with its infinite possibilities of self-destruction, is how to grow out of the world of armaments into a world of international security, based on law."

Dwight D. Eisenhower said: "We see as our goal not a superstate above nations, but a world community embracing them all, rooted in law and justice and enhancing the potentialities and common purposes of all peoples."

Arthur J. Goldberg, on assuming his post as chief of the United States mission to the United Nations, said: "There is simply no alternative in a nuclear age to world peace through the rule of law."

Pope John commented: "Today the universal common good poses problems...which cannot be adequately tackled or solved except by the efforts of public authorities which are in a position to operate in an effective manner on a worldwide basis."

If these bold statements frighten anyone, may I remind them of the words of Senator Arthur Vandenberg at the time of Senate ratification of the UN charter: "You may tell me that I have but to scan the present world with realistic eyes in order to see these fine phrases often contemptuously reduced to a contemporary shambles, that some of the signatories to this charter practice the precise opposite of what they preach even as they sign, that the aftermath of this war seems to threaten the utter disintegration of these ideals at the very moment they are born. I reply that the nearer right you may be in any such gloomy indictment, the greater is the need for the new pattern which promises at least to try to stem these evil tides."

I am proud to live where public authorities are courageously speaking out on behalf of an equal concern for all men everywhere, and in support of the concept of world citizenship in a world community of nations, living in peace under law.

(date is lost, but believed to be late 1968)

These remarks are from the speech I gave to two gatherings of the Junior Chamber of Commerce, or Jaycees, one in Minneapolis and one in St. Paul, within a span of three days in 1967:

⏭ Twenty-two years ago the United Nations organization came into being with four objectives: (1) to save succeeding generations from the scourge of war; (2) to re-affirm fundamental human rights; (3) to establish conditions under which justice and respect for international law can be maintained; (4) to promote social progress and better standards of life in larger freedom.

Despite a continuing power struggle among great nations, despite an over-use of the veto power, despite disputes over financing and despite many other problems large and small, the UN has survived, has grown in usefulness and remains today the world's best hope for universal peace.

As to its cost, our participation in the entire UN program amounted to 99 cents per capita in 1966. Our nation's expenditures for war, past, present and future, were over $300 per capita for the same year. For every penny we spend to promote world peace, we spend over $3 for war.

In its peacekeeping efforts, the UN has surely not done all that many have hoped would be possible. The main reason has been the desire of big powers to pursue unilateral courses, engage in regional alliances—in short, to use U.N. procedures only when it suited their purpose. In spite of these obstacles, over the past twenty-two years, the record shows numerous contributions to the averting of war, the easing of tensions, and the settling of disputes. There was Iran in 1946, Greece in 1947, Palestine in 1949, Korea in 1950, Suez in 1956, the Middle East in 1958, Cuba in 1962, West New Guinea in 1962, and each year since. Many of the efforts have been feeble and there have been varying degrees of success, but out of this body of experience come suggestions for the future I'll touch on shortly.

In pursuing its second, third and fourth objective, the UN has established or sponsored a large number of agencies carrying on a vast array of projects for the betterment of mankind. The work is done by thousands of volunteer and professional men and women of great talent and dedication, joined in a truly international civil service. The life of almost every person in the world is touched by one or another of these activities.

The United Nations Children's Fund (UNICEF) aids some fifty-five million children and mothers a year, in every part of the world. The United Nations High Commissioner for Refugees provides international protection for one and a half million refugees. The International Atomic Energy Agency established under the umbrella of the United Nations works to accelerate and enlarge the contribution of atomic energy to peace, health and prosperity throughout the world. The International Labor Organization negotiated agreements for improved minimum wages paid to seamen, and has organized a program to improve the living and working conditions of seven million Indians in the Andes of South America.

The Food and Agricultural Organization of the United Nations has 100 countries participating. Through the promotion of hybrid corn, the value of Europe's corn crop was increased 24 million dollars in one year. A cattle disease, the world's greatest killer of livestock, has been brought under control in some areas with a vaccine developed by FAO. The United Nations Educational, Scientific and Cultural Organization (UNESCO) has had many successes. UNESCO missions are at work in every part of the world advising governments on public education. Scientific and cultural exchanges are widespread. Under UNESCO peoples and nations have been brought together in cooperative effort on a broader scale than ever before in history.

The World Health Organization has effectively assisted countries fighting epidemics of malaria, TB, and other diseases by mass programs of vaccination and chemical spraying. Central America's malaria incidence, for example, was cut 50 percent in one year. The International Bank of Reconstruction and Development has made hundreds of loans totaling billions of dollars. The International Civil Aviation Organization has adopted standards for aircraft equipment, operating practices, to ensure safe and uniform conditions on civil flights everywhere. The Universal Postal Union fixes the cost of sending a letter from one country to another and works for faster and more efficient mail service. The International Telecommunications Union arranges different radio frequencies for different countries so they won't interfere with each other. The World Meteorological Organization is helping set up a network of weather stations all over the world.

This enormous range of global activity is infinitely greater than most citizens realize. It alone would justify everything we have invested in the UN.

I believe the idea of a world community—acceptance of the essential equality of humankind—accounts for success in the United Nations' social educational and cultural pursuits. UNICEF is a good example. The fundamental principle is that all children are equally precious—that all children everywhere are equally entitled to the benefits of food, shelter, clothing, family care, medicine, education and all the rest. The people from one nation working in this effort do not claim, insist upon, or really inwardly believe their children are somehow superior or more deserving.

There is no nationalism in UNICEF. In reviewing each of the UN agencies' work, it becomes evident that the degree of success is in direct proportion to the degree that nationalistic goals are set aside for concern about the well-being of all men everywhere. Once the concept of the brotherhood of men is truly accepted, there is a relaxation of tension and successful cooperation brings achievement.

What is developing today is an ever-increasing body of opinion that holds that we must look upon all the peoples of the world as one community that must find a way to operate under a body of world law to preserve peace.

I believe the time has come for the political leaders of the United States to institute such studies and actions towards changes in the United Nations structure as are necessary to make it a more effective lawmaking and peacekeeping body. Success will depend not so much upon the support of international idealists as upon the understanding scrutiny of pragmatists who neither exaggerate its present strength nor minimize its potential.

Among the matters to be considered would be:

1. Introducing a system of weighted voting into the structure, recognizing the reality of size, responsibility and potential contribution to international society of the member nations.
2. Consider universal membership, without expulsion nor withdrawal.
3. Acceptance of the United Nations charter as a constitution, and observance of its principles and use of its procedures as not a matter of diplomatic choice or convenience.
4. Review of court procedures and the whole law-making process.
5. Redouble efforts to have nations ratify the conventions so far adopted. Here the U.S. can show leadership. When President John F. Kennedy submitted the last three, he said, "The United States cannot afford to renounce responsibility for support of the very fundamentals, which distinguished our concept of government from all forms of tyranny."
6. Study renewed efforts for universal disarmament, save only for police forces for the internal requirements of each country, and a world police force under the direction of the United Nations and located strategically in various parts of the world.

These are some of the steps in a course that must be long and treacherous. Peace means more than the temporary absence of major war in an armed world. Genuine peace requires order and justice through enforceable world law. In short, peace requires government. In its absence, order and justice under the law cannot exist.

Out of this could truly come a new renaissance, a new spirit, and a new hope for all mankind everywhere. I believe in it and I want to work toward it not only because of its enormous possibilities, but also because of the utterly intolerable alternative.

—October 23 and 26, 1967

THE HOPE FOR DISARMAMENT

There was a brief time in the middle of the 1960s when Americans could dare to think that peace was at hand, and could turn their thoughts to disarmament. It was after the Cuban missile crisis of 1962 had passed, and a nuclear test ban treaty between the United States and the Soviet Union was signed in August 1963. During that period, as a former governor, I gave several speeches to state and national groups about the challenges and opportunities presented by disarmament.

Our hopes for disarmament were premature. Not long after this speech was given, the Vietnam War escalated. It was to be another generation before the Berlin Wall fell, the Soviet Union dissolved, and the Cold War ended. Disarmament finally came in the early 1990s, and brought with it a brief recession that was especially felt in areas where defense spending had been large. But by the mid-1990s the nation was experiencing unprecedented prosperity, proving what I predicted in the 1960s—that the nation need not spend lavishly on armaments to be economically healthy.

Still, the domestic investments I urged in 1965 were never made to the extent I believe they should have been. I submit that had the federal government turned its financial might on research, education, health care and other legitimate human needs after the Cold War ended, the nation would be stronger today. As I outlined then, the nation could have afforded both stepped-up domestic investments and a tax cut. Since then, politicians have claimed that the choice was one or the other, not both.

What has happened more recently has shown once again how fragile and fleeting peace and prosperity can be. In the wake of the terrorist attacks in New York and Washington of

September 11, 2001, the floodgates of spending on armaments have been opened. We're militaristic in our attack on terrorism and very defensive at home. We have declared war on terrorists wherever they may be found. We've even gone so far as to list the nations against which we could be expected to use nuclear weapons. We have said that we would undertake preemptive action instead of just defensive action. Indeed, that is how we justified war on Saddam Hussein's Iraqi government in 2003.

As a result, from a robust economy, we've gone to a deficit position in all of our governmental balance sheets. Expenditures on defense are being made at the expense of local needs. It's natural that the events of 9/11 would produce a strong reaction. But I still hope that we can achieve a balance that will both contain the risks we face in a dangerous world, and give the nation the domestic investment it deserves. The needs I spoke of in 1965 are greater than ever, and the consequences of ignoring them are graver than ever. Here is some of what I said:

⏭ At the first nationally televised teach-in, I heard one young man express concern about the suggestions for disarmament and peace. It was not out of fear for our national security, but our economic welfare. "Do you know what would happen," he rhetorically asked, "if our $50 billion defense industry were to shut off?"

Perhaps you have heard the story of Rosie the Riveter who worked in a West Coast shipyard during World War II. On lunch hour one day, she was heard to express decided reservations about the then Pope. When challenged, she explained that she and all her family had been unemployed until the defense boom came along and suddenly provided them with well-paying jobs. She said she found it hard to understand how the Pope, who was supposed to be a good Christian, could be praying, right out in public, for peace.

That story continues to reflect our economic involvement with national defense. Scores of articles have been written on the impact of disarmament with such titles as "Can Our Economy Stand Disarmament?" and "Could We Survive Peace?" emphasizing the pervasiveness of defense expenditures in our society. One writer devoted a book to "The Warfare State," developing in detail and with considerable alarm the degree to which the production of armaments influences our domestic and foreign policy decisions.

What is the extent of our defense operation? Obviously it is substantial, involving about 8 percent of our gross national product. Of the 1964 gross national product of $622 billion, the defense budget was $53 billion; of a 75 million-person labor force, 7.5 million people were in defense, 3.5 million in defense industries, 3 million in the armed forces and 1 million civilian employees in the Department of Defense. Of all men and women employed by government in the United States, federal, state and local, one of every three is employed by the Defense Department. That same department now supports more than one-third of the total research and development work now underway in the United States.

It is very significant that 80 percent of all industrial defense expenditures are concentrated in the aerospace-electronic-nucleonic-industrial complex. There is also a geographical concentration. In California, Washington, Kansas, Connecticut and New Mexico, 20 to 30 percent of all people in manufacturing work on defense. In the District of Columbia, Virginia, Alaska and Hawaii, one-tenth to one-fourth of all income is either military compensation, or Defense Department civilian wages and salaries.

Looking at individual communities, 82 percent of manufacturing workers in San Diego are in missiles and aircraft, 72 percent in Wichita, 53 percent in Seattle, 27 percent in Long Beach and Los Angeles. It is not difficult to understand how some people and communities can become committed to the necessity of large defense expenditures. Their economic welfare is bound up in them.

We must ask, to what extent is our current national posture of almost complete reliance on military strength in our foreign policy fostered by the vast establishment that depends on military expenditures for its existence? To what extent is fear of economic recession through reduction of military spending fostered by the same establishment? Have we anything to fear from our armament industry? If we could establish peace through world order under law, and vast reductions in military spending occurred, would we face insoluble economic problems? It is particularly to the last two questions that I would like to address myself.

When a president of the United States makes a farewell address, he can be depended upon to speak with the utmost conviction on a subject he believes paramount. No one could question the sincerity of President Eisenhower, or his acquaintance with military affairs and defense needs. In his farewell message delivered the evening of January 17, 1961, President Eisenhower discussed at length a "threat to democracy" new both in kind and degree, "the military-industrial complex," which he pictured as a colossus that had come to dominate vast areas of American life.

Until the latest of our world conflicts, he said, "the United States had no armaments industry. American makers of plowshares could, with time and as required, make swords as well. But we can no longer risk emergency improvisation of national defense. We have been compelled to create a permanent armaments industry of vast proportions...The total influence—economic, political, even spiritual—is felt in every city, every state house, every office of the federal government. Our toil, resources and livelihood are all involved; so is the very structure of our society.

"We must guard against the acquisition of unwarranted influence, whether sought or unsought, by the military-industrial complex. The potential for the disastrous rise of misplaced power exists and will persist. We must never let the weight of this combination endanger our liberties or democratic processes. Only an alert and knowledgeable citizenry can compel the proper meshing of the huge industrial and military machinery of defense with our peaceful methods and goals, so that security and liberty may prosper together."

This is a sober warning. It is hard to resist the financial demands of the armed forces based on their claims of military necessity and backed by the substantial economic interest of a giant industry. We are unlikely to get disarmament unless we are ready to embrace and vigorously advance an alternative to armament.

Any condition justifying disarmament must provide security for our people, protection for our sovereignty, and no interference with our individual freedom and liberty. Our people yearn for peace. The general satisfaction with the nuclear test ban agreement is an expression of it, even though we know the Russian record of violating any agreement whenever it is expedient to do so. Nevertheless, this treaty is a beginning of recognition that modern armaments are so dangerous that international control of their use is essential to everyone's welfare. So dangerous are nuclear weapons that no unilateral defense system can provide the basic security that is its only justification. The atomic weapons themselves thus may be the decisive factor inducing an international security system under enforceable international law as the best means of preserving our physical security and essential freedoms.

I look for disarmament to come, forced upon us by the threat of total destruction. I think we must work urgently and earnestly with like-minded nations to pound out the basic agreements essential to disarmament. In the long view, I share the optimism of Justice Oliver Wendell Holmes who said, "I think it probable that civilization somehow will last as long as I care to look ahead. I think it not improbable that man, like the grub that prepares a chamber for the winged thing it never has seen but is to be, that man may have destinies he does not understand, and beyond the vision of battling races and an improvised earth I catch a dreaming glimpse of peace."

—May 25, 1965

RELIGIOUS TOLERANCE

There are times when you speak, and something seems to take over. You say things you didn't anticipate saying. You draw from inner resources that you might not have known you had. That was what happened to me on October 4, 1993, when I was presented the David W. Preus Leadership Award at Luther Northwestern Seminary in St. Paul. Those who spoke before me were so generous and gracious that I thought I had better gather my wits about me and say something. Inasmuch as we were meeting in the chapel of the Lutheran Church, I thought it was a good time to make a point about the value of all religions, and the need to respect all religions.

That need has never been greater than it is today. Fundamentalist extremism and intolerance in almost every faith, including Christianity, have proven deadly, and could be devastating on a global scale. Americans need to ask why it is that we are hated by some religious people, who themselves are devoted to high ideals, but who feel we are so far wrong that we should be destroyed. We need to take seriously the answers. Religious understanding is not going to come about through warfare. It can only come about through sincere communication.

I began my remarks that day by paying tribute to my wife Eleanor. I have felt uneasy on more than one occasion when I was being praised, and her contributions went unmentioned. Eleanor has been central to every major decision I ever made. Her staying power, perseverance, wisdom, optimism and encouragement have been decisive factors for me, many times. She has been the inspiration and frequently the stabilization of my career. She is every bit as deserving, if not more, than I am.

When I spoke in 1993, I referred to our sixty-one years of marriage. This year, we observed our seventy-first anniversary. We frequently make mention of how lucky we have been to have each other, and to be together into advanced age. What a blessing it has been! Here is some of what I said at Luther Seminary:

⏭ I have been sitting here just dying to say one thing: "I wouldn't have amounted to a hill of beans without Eleanor Johnson." Only she knows the sacrifice that she has made so that activities could be carried forward. It's an exceedingly lucky man who can have sixty-one years of marriage with so wonderful a woman. I just thank you, Eleanor. None of this means anything except that it also reflects what you have done.

I thought of different ways of passing off some of the things that might be said today in a light manner, but I'm so deeply moved by what has been said that I find it hard to do that. Someone once said, "High praise is like fine perfume. It smells sweet but you aren't supposed to swallow it." I think I've been fortunate that the things I like to do were socially acceptable.

One thing I'm certainly aware of is that we're in a sacred place as we meet today. I think having a religious experience is fundamental to life. As we look ahead, I think it's terribly important that we try to avoid religious nationalism, where nations of one faith feel that they must impose themselves on other nations, and think that because they're acting out the mission of God, they have the right to do the most horrible things to accomplish their purpose.

To many of us here, the cross has a very special symbolism. To some of us who are here, it is not accepted. Can we find in a true religious faith an understanding that people can have a different commitment, and still be sincere, still have a part of the truth? How do we know but what there may be a universal truth, a universal faith, far beyond anybody's understanding? Each of us, in a way, is like the blind man with the elephant, reaching for a part of it, seeking to understand, quite sure of what we believe, but maybe only touching part of the truth. Can we accept that that is possible?

It would be a hideous future if we were to wind up using our age's great advances in communication and technology in the worst of all kinds of wars, religious war. Here where we have so much diversity, can we not find a greatness of spirit, so that however dedicated we may be to one belief, we somehow find it within ourselves to realize that others may also have great truth, as important to them as ours is to us? The fact is that in all faiths, there is a common denominator of love. There's a common denominator of caring about your neighbor. There's a common denominator of living beyond and outside one's self, that he who loses his life shall find it.

I've spoken to many Muslims—many of them cab drivers. We might think that their daily religious practices would become very routine and not very meaningful. My conversations have convinced me otherwise. Their daily rituals are very meaningful. Their faith is very serious. I think we need to learn to appreciate that.

We have entered a more global era. We can no longer think we can run a U.S. economy our way, greedy, rich, affluent, wasteful, while other nations all over the world live in poverty and people in hunger. It won't work. It's a political issue right now, relative to the North American Free Trade Agreement. Can we find it within ourselves to be as concerned to lift the standard of a Mexican peasant, as we are concerned about protecting our own welfare? Can we find that within ourselves? Must we be selfish? Must we be nationalistic? Must we be war-faring? If there is one governmental action that would please me tremendously, it is that we simply decide we are going to get out of the arms business and no longer sell arms to anybody. Rather, let's concentrate on defense, on research, stay strong, build the United Nations, work toward building a world that reflects our noblest beliefs but reflects respect for others' beliefs *equally*. That's very hard—to be as concerned for the welfare of people everywhere as we are with that of our own country's people. If we can, we could have a peaceful world.

The greatest accomplishment of the twentieth century was extending the life span of people by thirty years. If that continues, there are people being born today who will not only live in the twenty-first century but into the twenty-second. The potential for life, for beauty, for nobility is beyond all comprehension, if we can but give support to what we know to be the best of ourselves.

—October 4, 1993

TWO INTERVIEWS ABOUT INVOLVEMENT

When my autobiography, *A Man's Reach*, was published in 2000, I was interviewed on two occasions by Minnesota Public Radio, once by Gary Eichten, another time by Lorna Benson. They let me sound off on one of my favorite topics—the need for more people of wisdom and ability to become involved in government.

There is a great need in government for people who are unselfish, who have public service at heart, who have a capacity to see other people's viewpoints, and who seek a middle ground of compromise where there is a difference of opinion. Humankind must learn to get along together, and that requires a quality of leadership in government that we see too little of today. It is so crucial that people around the world become involved in governing themselves, and elect leaders who seek not self-aggrandizement, but service.

War is no solution to humanity's problems. It just breeds more hatred, more bloodshed, and more war. This nation's most recent venture in Iraq will, I fear, prove to be yet another violent exercise in futility. It was supposed to be a war over weapons of mass destruction, but none have appeared as yet. There was an assumption that the United Nations' orders were not being obeyed. The United States leapt to military action, when more inspections might have solved the problem.

Here are excerpts from the two MPR interviews:

⏭ Eichten: Governor, so many people say they just don't have time to get involved in public activities these days. They're running as fast as they can just to keep their personal life in order.

ELA: I think it's true. I think there are tremendous demands on families these days, with two family incomes and the school problems, the threats to young people, the difficulty of young people growing up. Things go on now that were unheard of when I was growing up as a boy. I think we've lost some of childhood, and live too fast, and consume life in gulps, rather than savoring its full taste. So, it is a difficult time. But, to me, the most important thing that people need to do is to make a decision. Once the decision is made and a commitment made, then other things can be worked out.

Eichten: Do people look outside themselves enough these days, Governor?

ELA: I think life is so absorbing these days that it's very hard. I think that's one of the advantages of old age: you're free of some of the moving around and some of the rush to meetings. You have time to sit and think. Sometimes you just sit. [laughter] But there's really opportunity to think and to review and to meditate, and that is a great pleasure.

Eichten: Governor, I know how much books mean to you. You've been collecting books for years, grand collections, and of course, now, we have the Elmer L. Andersen Collection at the university. It must be tough not being able to actually read anymore.

ELA: Oh, that's tough. But, it always is true that no matter what happens, there are always alternatives. No matter what happens, you have to look to see what advantage you can get out of it. The fact of the matter is, there are all kinds of services to aid visually impaired people. I get books on tape. Many people now use that in their cars traveling around to work and other places. There are 155,000 books on tape in the Library of Congress that are available. I get *Newsweek* every week on tape. There's a single channel radio station that's twenty-four hours a day reading magazine articles, newspaper coverage, and books. Then my dear wife reads to me a good deal. We're reading right now a book on Luther's theology. We previously finished reading the life of Warren Magnuson [*Warren G. Magnuson and the Shaping of Twentieth-Century America* by Shelby Scates], the senator from Washington. We don't have enough time to make the most of all the opportunities there are. I think that's true of life in general, that no matter what happens, if you dig around, you'll find an alternative.

—Sept. 7, 2000

* * * *

Benson: Where would you like to see politics go in the future?

ELA: I'd like to see more people participate and use [the politcal process] to obtain change. I don't like to see protests and violence and angry people shouting out of frustration. We live in a wonderful democracy that has all the techniques available to get change. People just need to organize. It's hard work. It's hard work to want to have a voice in the legislature and give up whatever else you're doing and take time from your family and serve in the legislature. But, it's a wonderful experience, a very satisfying experience. We're so fortunate in this country of freedom and opportunity that we can make a difference. One person can make a difference.

Benson: For those who remember you or know you primarily in your political life, what do you want people to know about you?

ELA: Well, I'd like to have them know that I tried to be fair and that I love this country. I feel *so* privileged to be a part of the United States of America. I love Minnesota and I love the University of Minnesota. I guess I'd like people to know that love is the really great compelling force in life, whether it's personal love, love for a country, love for an issue, dedication to something that you care about so wholeheartedly that you'd even give your life for it. That, I think, is the ultimate realization and fulfillment of life.

—August 16, 2000

THE NEW WORLD ORDER

Charlie Boone of WCCO Radio in the Twin Cities has been a dear friend for many years. Some of the most sparkling times I had were when I would go on WCCO's *Boone & Erickson*, with Charlie and his longtime partner, Roger Erickson. I would not have the slightest idea what they were going to ask me, so I would have to be prepared for anything, and always in a good sense of humor, because the program was to be entertaining as well as informative. Out of that came a friendship that goes on to this day.

Charlie and I were without Roger in early 1992 when we discussed the momentous world events of the year that had just passed—the first Persian Gulf War, the continuing breakup of the old Soviet empire, and worldwide economic doldrums. We found time for some personal topics too. Here are excerpts from my on-air interview with Charlie:

CB: I've always said that Elmer L. Andersen is probably one of the greatest resources this state has. You have given us so much in all the things you do.

ELA: Thank you, Charlie.

CB: Of course, you've been an executive. H.B. Fuller Company for many years, you were CEO, and you publish a newspaper. How many papers do you publish now?

ELA: Seven.

CB: Seven! And, you got into that kind of late, which is great news for people who are maybe in the years where they're thinking of retirement. You were in your retirement years, and got busier.

ELA: I always think of Doctor [Laurence] Gould down at Carleton. When our son was visiting there, he asked him, a high school student, what he planned to do with his life. Dr. Gould was then nearing retirement. Our son was a little uneasy, not really knowing what he wanted to do, and to put him at ease, Dr. Gould said, "Julian, don't be upset if you don't know what you want to do yet. I'm not sure what I want to do." I think all of us should think in terms of continual activity and living and learning and loving, and just having a wonderful time in this world of ours.

CB: We're great admirers of you because you're a lifelong learner. Learning is probably the most invigorating activity that we take part in.

ELA: It certainly is. This morning, early this morning, I was rereading Rachel Carson's book, *The Sense of Wonder*. If there's anything that people might well try to retain, it's just the curiosity and the interest about all the things that are right at our beck and call: nature and the stars, the trees, and just life, just the mystery and the miracle of life in all of its aspects. Even just being aware of that is a great satisfaction in our life.

CB: There's so much right around us.

ELA: So much right around us. We both love books and we can have friends...I've had the fun of picking out my own ancestors. Instead of running down my own genealogy, through the love of books, I've picked some great characters like Erasmus during the time of the Reformation and William Morris in the nineteenth century and Jonathan Carver in our own Minnesota. You know, you can really build up a marvelous genealogy if you can pick them out yourself.

CB: They make great friends.

EA: Oh, they make great friends, and you can really have a sense of friendship through books, through the love of books and reading. There's no finer heritage for young children than having books read to them by their parents. Parents should read to their children.

CB: We like to bash TV. Families, generally, that are a little stricter on their television watching for their children tend to read more.

ELA: There are wonderful things on TV and, certainly, it can be used, but it should be limited and controlled. It just shouldn't be aimless and many hours a day of just sitting at the TV. There should be activity and hiking and exploring and learning about nature in all sorts of ways. You know, you can just take a cup of water out of a pond and watch it. Life in a cup of water out of a pond, can be a marvelous mystery developing for young children.

CB: I've always admired you for your enthusiasm and zest for life. You have an inner youth that is marvelous.

ELA: You know, there's an interesting thing about the word enthusiasm. It comes from a Greek word *enthos*, e-n-t-h-o-s, which means the God within. I think that's a marvelous heritage for that word. When you see people that are enthusiastic, it makes you feel kind of good.

CB: It sure does.

ELA: I love people who are enthusiastic about what they do and if they can't be, they ought to change what they do. Life is too short to be bored and dull and pedestrian. Life can be exciting.

CB: I thought of you immediately when we were doing our year-end reviews. I thought, I'd love to call Elmer and say, "This past year has been such a momentous year."

ELA: Tremendous. It certainly must be, will be, recorded as one of the most momentous years of this century, with the breakdown of the Soviet Union and the reestablishing of these republics. I'm so glad it worked out. I thought we were pursuing a little of the wrong slant, it seemed to me, by trying to preserve the Soviet Union through [Premier Mikhail] Gorbachev, when all these republics were struggling for freedom. I hope, now that the die has been cast and the republics are establishing themselves, that we help them succeed. I just think it's a tremendous thing.

Then, of course, the Persian Gulf War was just awesome in the demonstration of U.S. military technology and the tremendous personnel. It was just an incredible demonstration. There, again, just as one person, I still feel, and felt at the time, that we should have waited and identified our goal a little better because, now, we recognize that just freeing Kuwait didn't really accomplish a great deal. Saddam Hussein may be more powerful than ever. He should have been the objective, and it's too bad that our strategy was a little flawed, it seems to me. Of course, hindsight is always so much better than having to make the decisions on the run.

Nineteen ninety-one was a tremendous year, but really mainly I think years are individual. A big event for us is the birth of our first great grandchild. That's a very personal thing. I don't know how earth shaking it will be. But, I must say, it's amazing, after all the billions of children that are born, how much improvement can still be made.

I think, to a great extent, people build their own universe. They make their own lives. I think if people build their future, it will come true. If they wait for it to happen, it just may not happen or it may not be very interesting. I think 1992 will be what people decide they're going to make it. I think attitude and feelings about things and just loving life and loving to live it and even recognizing that in disappointments, there can be opportunity and challenge... I look toward 1992 with enthusiastic optimism and if tough things happen, that will be part of our challenge and an opportunity to show what we can do about it. We have a lot of problems, but I don't think there are any that are not within our capacity to solve.

CB: I was at a wedding in Iowa and a family was there that was just back from Singapore, where they had been working for a multinational U.S. company. Now, they're adjusting to almost a cultural shock coming back here. One of the things they talked about was the fear of their security in a big city, as opposed to Singapore where there is complete safety. There are other places around the world where it is safe, where there is very little crime, where there are no drugs. How unfortunate in this great country, which has so much potential and has so many good things, that we do have some things that diminish our quality of life and our safety.

ELA: I think we've lost some sense of value. Life has been speeded up too much for young people. They get into experiences of life that might be much better delayed. Then, after a while, they've explored everything, and then they have to get artificial stimulants to keep the hype up. It's out of gear, surely. It's puzzled me why drugs that have been available for centuries, all of a sudden, have become of such epidemic proportions in our own country. I think it reflects something on our value system, how we're running our lives and how we're spending our time. I think there is going to have to be some reappraisal, and I think some of that is going on now. I think people are reconsidering what's important to them and what objectives should really be. We've become a very materialistic society, and maybe we're going to get away from that and get back to some more fundamental values.

CB: There's a lot of unemployment today and a lot of unhappiness, homelessness, and a lot of problems that we have to think about. It's no picnic, obviously, for people in trouble.

ELA: No, it certainly isn't. Probably the greatest challenge is to try to find balance. We need certain economic success in order to be able to provide for family and have the things that we enjoy in life. But, at the same time, if that becomes too dominant, then it gets out of gear relative to giving the family the attention it should have. Then, there is the community. One of the great challenges in our society right now is the indifference toward the government, the feeling that government is expensive and wasteful, so people don't vote. They feel turned off. They feel they can't make a change. All of that is not very good. I favor and am happy about getting the presidential preference primary back. I don't think people should be required to disclose their party preference. I hope they amend that out of the law. But, anything that would stimulate people's interest in government, I think would be good. We need a balance between community concerns, church concerns, family concerns, business concerns and finding that balance, that might well be the challenge for everybody in 1992.

CB: We were talking about the events of 1991. The Communist republics under the Soviet Union falling and changing over to a more democratic form of government and changing over to market economy, that's got to be a difficult thing to do in a short time.

ELA: It certainly is. Nothing would be more helpful than to have certain of the supply lines get filled up, particularly food and clothing. The news is filled with long lines of people waiting and then the tremendously high prices. If something could be done to just fill up those supply lines and give democracy a chance to get going...because people won't stand for paying half or two-thirds of their month's salary for a pound of beef. I think we have a lot at stake to make the new republics work, to help them make it work.

CB: A year ago, we moved men and materiel over to the Persian Gulf with the war happening. It seems that same kind of technology and effort could be used. We have warehouses full of butter and cheese that could be used over there.

ELA: Oh, yes. If we use the same all-out crisis approach to peaceful efforts that we do wartime efforts...Certainly, they're appropriate in wartime, but in peacetime, if we would right now just be having shiploads, planeloads, of food of all kinds...my goodness, that would stimulate our local agricultural economy. It would certainly aid over there. I think it should be done through agencies that we can depend on like the Red Cross and others. Somehow, to just stand by and see if they're going to make it is really not the role the United States should be playing. We were really too slow to recognize the Baltic countries, kind of slow recognizing these new republics. We ought to get with it and recognize that we have a lot at stake in the success of the Ukraine and all of them.

CB: Why does it take so long to react to things? It seems we're always reacting instead of planning ahead. Is government built that way in this country?

ELA: Government moves slowly, but I'm afraid there's also the issue of the objectives that are involved. It takes, really, an altruistic approach of wanting to *give* rather than wanting to get. Frequently, I think, when we do act quickly, it's because we clearly see our own self-interest and then act to protect it or enhance it. I just think we need a more altruistic approach, realizing what the United States has to give. To pay up our dues at the United Nations, to support the United Nations, to get with making peace work around the world—that, to me, I think would be an exciting challenge for 1992 and the new century. This had been a century of war. Almost all of the economies that have prospered have been a result of wartime expenditures. I just wish we could demonstrate the economic value of peacetime activities.

CB: Is that going to be difficult in 1992 because of our election year? Is that going to make people have a different agenda?

ELA: I heard one economist say, "We've been a long time getting into the difficulty we're in and we're not going to get out of it overnight." Yet, the [George H.W. Bush] administration clearly will be looking for some quick fix that will get the public satisfied so there can be a reelection of the present administration. Then there's a desire on the other side, of course, to try and maximize the difficulties. There's an awful lot of politics involved in everything in 1992. But, I think that once the people speak up, and if people could only realize how important they are individually in their letters, their phone calls, their participation, they can make such a big difference. They've put presidents right out of office. When public opinion crystallizes and mobilizes, it has incredible power. All it is, is just a sum total of individuals. So, if individuals would decide what we ought to be doing and how we ought to be doing it and let their will be known, that's the most powerful force in our country.

CB: More participation by the citizens?

ELA: More participation and personal concern with things beyond oneself...to think beyond one's own self and think, I want to build a better community. I want to build a better state. I want to be part of a strong, helpful nation. I want to be in a world that is concerned about people everywhere, knowing that it isn't going to be very safe to have joy and happiness anywhere, if it isn't available pretty much for people everywhere.

CB: What would you like to see for the new year?

ELA: Well, I would like to see the United States pay up its dues to the United Nations, recognize the role of the United Nations, and be generously open-hearted, as our people can certainly be, in getting food and clothing wherever in this world it's needed, to give freedom a chance.

CB: Elmer L. Andersen, former governor, and publisher of many newspapers, and a great citizen of this state of Minnesota. Good to see you. Happy New Year.

ELA: Happy New Year to you, Charlie, and wonderful to be with you. Thanks so much.

—January 6, 1992

AFTER SEPTEMBER 11

Every year, the Minnesota Supreme Court hosts a forum for representatives of the state's legislative and judicial branches, to promote mutual understanding of each other's work. I was honored in December 2001 when Chief Justice Kathleen Blatz invited me to deliver the keynote address at the forum. I have long considered the judiciary the most important of the three branches of American government. It is the part of government that is most immutable to change, and most potent in its ability to secure the rights we cherish as Americans.

I spoke that day out of concern about the erosion of those rights in the period after the attack on the Pentagon and the World Trade Center on September 11, 2001, just three and a half months before. My feeling is stronger today that we need to protect our civil rights, and not go overboard in our reaction to a terrible deed. I think the Bush administration overreacted in the months that followed those attacks. There have been many problems, hurts and failures that affect more people than were destroyed on 9/11. Terrible as it was, there are situations that are more terrible that go comparatively unnoticed. This was an act of brazen, unprecedented aggression, and that is why it got a strong reaction. I tried to warn in the speech to the state's judiciary against giving terrorists the victory of destroying our own civil rights, as we react to the horror of that event.

I disagreed with President Bush's decision to invade Iraq without provocation in the spring of 2003. Bush's decision to invade had nothing to do with defending the United States against terrorism. There was no evidence that Iraq had any tie with the perpetrators of the attacks in New York City and Washington. The threat from North Korea is more real and more obvious, and there's no proposal of war there. The president had other motivations. I suspect that one of them was control of oil. The war was also a political opportunity to capitalize on the post— 9/11 attitude of the country, which is of a mind to poke at any perceived enemy or threat that comes within range.

A healthier response to 9/11 would have been for the United States to begin an aggressive policy of oil conservation, and a development of alternative energy sources. When I was in high school, there was an electric car in Muskegon, Michigan. I thought, what a profound advance that was! It moved so silently and gracefully around town. Everybody admired that electric car. And yet we have not progressed toward that technology. There has been an assumption that Americans are unwilling to pay a premium for safety and protection of the environment. I would love to see entrepreneurs challenge that assumption.

In the days before U.S. forces invaded Iraq, thousands of people descended on Washington DC to protest the rush to war. I was heartened to see it. In this country, the people usually come out on top eventually. There will be periods of darkness, and seeming inattention to basic issues, but the United States has a pretty good record over the long haul. The people are sometimes slow to be aroused. But once aroused, they move with force and clarity, and keep the country as bright as it is. It is still the beacon of the whole world. Here is some of what I said in December 2001:

⏭ I have the most profound respect for the judiciary. I think the judiciary is the bulwark that protects the rights of each American citizen. It's the court of last resort for everybody. There's an enormous sense of security in having good, reliable courts. There was no duty that I had as governor that commanded more attention than appointing judges. I was anxious that they be good. I thought to start a person on a judicial career was important, to get people that had the potential to be on the Supreme Court, and encourage the idea of a career in the judiciary. So, I am pleased from that standpoint to be here.

I wasn't going to ask if you could hear me. I was once speaking in a long narrow hall and started to speak and someone at the rear stood up and said, "We can't hear you." So, I tried to project and raise my voice and a second person got up and said, "I can't hear you." Whereupon, somebody who was sitting right in front stood up and turned around and said, "Well, I can. I'll trade places with you." So, if you can't hear me, you may be more fortunate than you know.

Kathleen—I can't help but be a little personal—asked me to comment on a couple of things. One was an interest all of you display in homeland security, and the new issues we face as a result of September 11. It's a little hard to say anything, because it was such a disaster that almost anything that is done as a result is acceptable. But I think there are some warnings that ought to be put out, and the judiciary is the important place in which to do that, as well as the legislature. Politics enters into everything, and political advantage is sought out of every situation. You have to recognize that. So legislation adopted as an excuse generated by September 11 is not always worthy. I think there are two examples. I think there are unreasonable benefits for big business being suggested, tax cuts and so on, at a time when there's going to be a shortage of funds. And I think the whole matter of human rights is terribly important.

My own philosophy of human relationships was relatively simple. I long ago decided that there was a lot of good in everyone. I've known people from every stratum of life, and there's good potential in every single human being I've known. But, also, I'm frank to admit, there's the possibility of evil in every single human being. There are none of us that are perfect. So, what's the solution? The solution is to try to put people into an environment where they're encouraged to be at their best. When you have homeless children and deprived portions of the civilization and discrimination and lack of affordable housing, you don't put people in a position to be at their best.

I think we've gone a little overboard on criminal punishment. I think we need to have a little more emphasis on rehabilitation. There are studies that have been made that show, without exception, that incarceration beyond six months is of very little benefit in rehabilitation, and can amplify a problem rather than help solve it. Yet it's been very popular to be tough on crime. We have the highest percentage of our population in incarceration of any progressive nation in the world. So, being tough on crime needs a little consideration.

I think that we need to support the administration in its efforts at combating terror. But I also think we have to be careful that we don't give the terrorists a victory by too many changes in our own human rights. I think the issue of military tribunal is one that should bear very close attention. We should protect the Bill of Rights, and not let an incident, tragic as it is, sacrifice fundamentals of our own belief and our own character. It took a great deal of planning over a long period of time to carry out that incident. We shouldn't overreact and expect that there's a bomb around every corner. But, we do need to be more alert. Certainly, it would seem that if somebody comes into a flight training school and wants to learn how to fly a plane but not to take it off or not to land it, that ought to create a little concern on somebody's part as to what objective the person has in mind. If somebody comes to talk about crop dusting, we need to be more alert. That can be done on a neighborhood basis. We had Neighborhood Watch in our neighborhood so that if anything out of the ordinary happened or if there seemed to be prowlers around, they'd be reported. Every citizen can make a contribution to greater care and greater support. So, while giving our leaders the support they need to carry on a difficult mission, we shouldn't go overboard in restricting fundamental rights of our own people. It's going to be a difficult time.

It was one thing to have twenty years of economic growth. Now, we're heading into a recession, and we don't know how long or how deep it may be. I was married in 1932. I talked to my sales manager and asked him if we could have a week off the first week in September because I was getting married. He said, "You're getting married, Elmer? This is no time to take on any new responsibility. We can't even guarantee you a job, to say nothing of the pay you're now receiving." I said, "Ed, I didn't ask you for marriage counseling. I just asked you for a week off in September. We're getting married. The Depression is going to have to take care of itself."

I think there's a certain American spirit that is called forth by necessity, frequently in trying situations. There was a fire that burned a church in Minneapolis, and the pastor had reason to say that there had never been such unity in the congregation as there was brought about by that fire. So, it's been another part of my own belief that in every incident, there's something to be learned. When something happens that seems to be a tragedy or a disappointment, there is something to turn to advantage. So, I think it is now, that if we can capitalize on the great show of affection for the country, the great display of the flag, by transmitting that to participation in elections, and the realization that any person can make a difference, any person can add to the culture of the country, any person can add to the happiness of the unfortunate. If we all do what we can where we can, then we'll have a good country. I think it was Eisenhower who said, "America will be great as long as she is good. If she ever ceases to be good, she'll cease to be great."

—December 18, 2001

VI. FUNDAMENTALS

MAPS

There are many ways people can exercise their citizenship, but there's no more effective way than being a member of the legislature and working for legislation that brings needed change. I loved being a legislator. Right from my first session, in 1949, I had the sense that I was part of making decisions and finding answers. I was responsible for more legislation than any other senator in 1949.

I was particularly pleased about the topographical mapping legislation, because that need had been neglected for so many years. In 1949 Minnesota was one of the least-mapped states in the country. Because of the bill I sponsored in my first session, we now have some of the best mapping of our territory. Obtaining the maps was not a great expense. The U.S. Geological Survey prepared them and stood a portion of the cost. It was just a matter of the legislature being awakened to the need. That is often what it takes to solve problems. Lack of awareness is often one of the biggest obstacles to improvement.

The mapping bill was one that young people could readily appreciate. Here is some of what I said about it to the Ramsey County Young Republican annual convention in North St. Paul, just after the 1949 session adjourned:

⏭ The Mapping and Topographic Survey Bill provided an appropriation of $50,000 a year for the next two years, to be matched by a similar amount from the U.S. Geological Survey, to produce maps in Minnesota.

Let me give you a little background: Many years ago, Congress appropriated money to the U.S. Geological Survey to be used to match appropriations of the state governments, dollar for dollar, to produce topographical maps. For a great many years, thirty-five or forty, the various states have been carrying on the work, and forty of the forty-eight states are currently carrying on the mapping project. Wisconsin, for example, has been appropriating $45,000 per year and is currently 60 percent mapped; North Dakota has been appropriating $16,000 a year, and is nearly completely mapped.

Minnesota, up to the present legislature, had appropriated no money for nearly twenty years and is only 9 percent mapped, ranking forty-ninth in the United States and territories. Consider: our territory and state have been legal entities for 100 years, and still only 9 percent of the area of the state has been adequately and officially mapped! Even Hawaii [not yet a state] has a higher percentage of its area mapped than has Minnesota! For all these years, Minnesota taxpayers have been paying federal taxes, a portion of which have been used to subsidize this mapping project in other states, and we here have been doing nothing to take advantage of this program. Bills have been introduced at several legislative sessions to no avail. Last fall Governor [Luther] Youngdahl appointed a commission to make an exhaustive survey, and it came up with a comprehensive report that was the foundation for the legislation that was enacted at the session just closed.

The procedure is a simple one. When a state has appropriated money for the purpose, it so notifies the U.S. Geological Survey. They appropriate an amount comparable to the state appropriation, and then their personnel begin work. In our state the project is under the direction of the commissioner of conservation, aided by an advisory board whose main function is to determine the areas of the state to be mapped, and in what order. Areas are taken by quadrangles of thirteen miles east and west and seventeen miles north and south. The maps are on a scale of one inch to the mile and the elevations are charted on contour lines for every ten feet of variations in elevation. The staff of the U.S. Geological Survey locates the official boundary lines of all governmental subdivisions, charts the precise location of lakes, streams, railroads, highways, and then determines elevations for the contour lines. When the survey work is complete, the Geological Survey, at its expense, produces the plates and prints the maps, so actually the overall cost of the project is divided about 60 percent with federal funds, 40 percent with local funds.

How are the maps used? Nothing is so fundamental to any economic project as a dependable map. For example, if there is to be a soil erosion study or project in any part of the state, the first need is for a good topographical map. Any study that the aeronautics commission makes in reference to airfield locations in the state depends first on the study of topographic maps, of which none have been available. The Highway Department must have maps to chart new locations for highways or straighten out existing highways.

During the war, the proposal was made that Camp Ripley be enlarged. The first requirements were topographical maps to send to Washington for their consideration. None were available, and because of the time it would take to produce satisfactory maps, the whole project was dropped. At least two large chemical industries were considering locating sizable plants on the Mississippi River, between St. Paul and La Crosse, Wisconsin, and required as a foundation of their consideration topographical maps for study, to determine the adaptability of the sites to the particular operation under consideration. When maps were not available, and time and expense could not be spent obtaining the necessary information, the projects went elsewhere.

It was one of my most satisfying experiences in the legislature that I could be the main author on this mapping bill in the Senate. We are far, far behind other states, but at least we are now underway.

—April 22, 1949

BARBERS

I had a very dear friend named Ed Hall, an African American. He and his brother had a barbershop in St. Paul that was a gathering place for politicians, and hence a great place to go to get the news. Political news of all kinds was brought there and disseminated there. Ed was a leader in St. Paul's African American community. He helped found Hallie Q. Brown settlement house and the St. Paul chapter of the NAACP. He was also active in the state Barbers' Association.

I was invited to speak to the state barbers' convention in 1957, when Ed Hall was the organization's secretary. That was no mere title. Ed went around the state, visiting with other barbers, asking about mutual problems, discussing prices, and generally running the organization. He was a peacemaker and a go-between among all the barbers. A controversy among them in those years was whether people trained as barbers in prison should be granted licenses. Ed worked to soothe the resentment some barbers felt toward those newcomers to their profession.

I commented at the convention on the price of a haircut, which was always a topic of lively discussion among barbers. I'm sure Ed had something to do with my opinion on that question. Here's what I said:

⏭ Since our local shops increased the price of haircuts from $1.50 to $1.75, there has been a good deal of discussion on haircut prices. Some people have even been moved to write letters of complaint to the newspapers, and this has brought some letters of irritated defense from the barber trade.

My observation is that barbers charge the least of any related profession or skilled craft. Let's make some comparisons. The first I don't offer in complete seriousness, but the fact is that the barber does about everything a psychiatrist does, and cuts hair in the bargain. The patient is put in a comfortable position, encouraged to relax and feel self-satisfied, and then to talk about anything that is on his mind, unload his grief and problems, and seek advice. The barber, like the psychiatrist, is required to be knowledgeable on any subject the patient may bring up. After a half hour of listening the psychiatrist makes a few observations, and then charges at least $15. 00. The barber does all of this, cuts the hair also, and charges $1. 75.

I wonder how much legal advice one could get for $1.75, or what the reaction would be to requesting a doctor to make a $1.75 treatment. If you asked a plumber for a $1.75 service call, he would probably tell you that that would not be enough to get him to your house. I am reminded of the lady who called a plumber to repair her washing machine. He came and quickly found a loose connection, tightened a nut and went on his way. Shortly thereafter the housewife received a bill for $8.20. She was very much concerned and called for an explanation. The plumber was very nice about it, and said he would send an itemized statement. In a few days, along came the statement listing "for tightening nut—20 cents," and on the next line, "for knowing which nut to tighten—$8.00." A reasonable person would have to conclude that haircuts are under-priced at $1.75.

Just what does a barber do for his fee? He does much more than simply cut hair.

Here are a few of the services rendered that occur to me offhand:

1. The barber keeps his place open, ready to extend service, whenever a customer wants to use it. This is mighty costly all by itself.

2. A good barbershop provides reading matter, and it is becoming very up-to-date reading matter.

3. The modern barbershop maintains sanitation, and that is very important. It really isn't so long ago that "barber's itch" was a common hazard of visiting a barbershop. In spite of the many people served every day, I cannot even recall when I last heard of anyone picking up any kind of infection from a visit to a barbershop. When you stop to think of it, that is a tremendous record in itself.

4. The barbershop provides clean linen. You visit the lavatory of a modern hotel, and the attendant expects to get anything from 10 cents to a quarter for the use of one small hand towel. Think of the linen cost in the modern barbershop, where every customer served can require several towels.

5. The barber cuts the hair, following all the latest styles and trends, to please the taste of every individual. No mass production job does this.

6. He listens patiently to the customers talk, whatever it might be.

7. He supplies the latest information on all subjects that comes to him.

8. Finally, he sends his customer away rested, relaxed, looking nicer, with a new sense of well-being, and even smelling good. All of this for $1.75! It really ought to be twice as much.

—September 15, 1957

MY LOVE OF BOOKS

Books have always held a great attraction for me. They provide the best way to communicate in a lasting way, generation after generation. They are not impeded by changes in technology, in the way that other media can be. For example, there have been three or four major changes in recording technology in my lifetime. Victrola records cannot be played on a modern compact disc player. But books are always useful. If one can have and hold an original edition, the original form of a book, just as an author saw it and planned it, one can commune with that author. That makes a lasting impression.

In 1997, I was given the Kay Sexton leadership award by the Minnesota Book Awards, a program of the Minnesota Humanities Commission. It prompted an interview with Patrick Coleman, the Minnesota Historical Society's acquisition librarian and host of the cable TV program Northern Lights. Here is some of what I said on that program about the value of books:

⏭ Coleman: What began your love of reading and your love of books and your book collecting?

ELA: I had an aunt who was a schoolteacher. We used to like to go over to her house because she had books. One set of books she had was "Journeys through Book Land." This was when I was a boy, a little boy. It was selections from famous children's literature. I just loved that set of books. I have a set now, in fact, *the* set that she had many years ago. That was a beginning.

Then, different individuals...One individual who influenced me a good deal was Desiderius Erasmus, a Reformation scholar. He appealed to me so much because, in a time of turmoil, he didn't want to leave the Catholic Church. He didn't want to oppose it. He was a priest. He saw its deficiencies and he was critical of it, but he wanted to resolve things. I think conflict resolution has appealed to me in public life and in private life.

Coleman: How young were you when you started reading Erasmus?

ELA: Oh, I didn't read the *Praise of Folly*, I'm sure, until I was in high school or college. But, I became aware of him as a person quite early, because I was a Lutheran. I admired Luther for what he stood for, but I thought he was a little too contentious. That's why I liked Erasmus.

Coleman: When you were first starting to read, were you getting books out of the public library?

ELA: I was getting some books out of the public library. Somehow, I liked the idea of having books for reference, for rereading and just the feeling you have about being around books. I think books have an ambience like a cathedral. They just *do* something for you. Back of me on the shelf here used to be the journal of Ralph Waldo Emerson. It just pleased me to know that any time I wanted to, I could have a morning visit with Ralph Waldo Emerson or Oliver Wendell Holmes, the great autocrat of the breakfast table. I just love the *feeling* of books, as well as the reading of them.

Coleman: When did you start collecting books and what were the first books that you collected?

ELA: Somewhere quite early on, I became aware of an English historian named James Anthony Froude. He was the leading historian at one time during the nineteenth century, but he wrote many other books. He wrote one little set of books, "Short Studies on Great Subjects," that appealed to me. I haven't been much interested in fiction, with a few exceptions; Edith Wharton, Storm Jameson, Ellen Glasgow, Willa Cather are some exceptions. They all happen to be women. There are some good men novelists also. But, mainly, I read non-fiction, history, biography. Biographical studies have always interested me a great deal.

Then, I got into the history of books themselves, books about books, books on libraries, books on book collectors, books on printing, books on paper, books on ink, books on type, everything about a book. It's quite a field of collecting called "Books about Books." That became a major area. Books on Minnesota became a major area. I was pleased to come upon the journal of Colonel Snelling that he kept out at Fort Snelling. That was maybe one of the most unique books I ever had, because it was the only one of its kind. It was his own journal.

Coleman: There's some debate going on now about the future of books. I think that you articulate, probably better than anybody

I know, why books are still important or, in this age of digital information, why they will persist.

ELA: Every time there has been a new communication development, it was going to sweep everything else aside. I can remember, as a child, when radio came. People would stay up all night as they now stay up all night on the Internet, seeing all the places they can get and all the people they can be in touch with. We used to tune in KDKA-Pittsburgh, WGN-Chicago, and to Kansas City Nighthawks and everybody kept a log. Radio was going to eliminate everything. TV was going to eliminate everything. Movies were going to be dead. Books were going to be gone. The fact of the matter is that the expansion of communication just expands the use of communication. There are more books being published today than have ever been published. A lot of people go to theaters. A lot of people watch TV. There's cable TV that serves a wonderful function. We watch CNN and C-SPAN. There's just so much today that there isn't enough time for everything. But, books are going to be around because there's just something about holding a book and communing with the author, particularly if you get into a first edition. The feeling that you had the book in the very form, maybe the very copy, that the author himself handled, that's a thrilling thing, particularly if the author died a couple hundred years ago. Oh, I think books are here to stay.

—May 1997

CIVIL DISOBEDIENCE AND THE RULE OF LAW

In 1984, at a convention in Moorhead, Minnesota, the American Lutheran Church took up a policy statement that greatly concerned me as an active lay member of the denomination. It was a statement outlining the church's understanding of the relationship Lutherans had to civil law. In its early drafts, it seemed to me to make overly broad allowances for disregard for the law when Christians in good conscience disagree with it. I thought the church was going off on a tangent, meaning well but striking at the heart of the rule of law of this country.

I was not a delegate, but I drove to Concordia College, where the convention was in progress, and asked to speak. The result was a message that has application not only to the policy document that was being considered by the Lutherans, but to Americans of conscience in other times and places.

In societies where there is no fair rule of law, where there is tyranny and oppression, the only solution is revolution. Thomas Jefferson said that when democracy fails and freedoms are taken from the people, there comes a point at which revolution is the only alternative.

But in our country, I hate to see people opt for trespass or other violation of the law. A lawful means of correction is available to them. I said as much as chairman of the Board of Regents at the University of Minnesota in the 1970s, when students protested the war in Vietnam. I told the protesters that if they had any complaint and they wanted to speak to the Board of Regents, they could do so anytime. They could request a hearing, and it would be granted. But they could not interfere with the learning process of others. That was a violation of the rights of others, and would not be tolerated.

The legal rights Americans enjoy are so precious that we should guard against losing them under the pressure of an unusual situation, such as the fear that swept the nation after the World Trade Center and Pentagon attacks of September 11, 2001. When people are under duress, they might thoughtlessly give away freedoms that are terribly important. As Americans, we do well to ground ourselves in understanding of and appreciation for our rule of law, so that we have confidence in it when we need it most.

Here is some of what I said that day in Moorhead:

⏭ What a person does on his or her own initiative out of deeply held conviction is a personal decision that I respect. If a law is violated, there will be penalties. That person should not be abandoned by the church. But others should not be encouraged to follow that route, because in our country, there is a better way.

One of the kinds of law violation under discussion is that of congregations providing sanctuary for undocumented persons, also identified as illegal aliens. This is a serious matter. I wonder if any congregation feels it is truly competent to determine the status of refugees from other nations, and to operate outside the law of our country, which is the most considerate of aliens seeking haven of any nation on earth. Federal laws provide for the acceptance of alien people who would be persecuted in their native countries, based on the long-established principle of political asylum.

If there are any abuses or discriminatory decisions by immigration administration officials, those people should be removed, so that the laws will be correctly enforced. Congress has power to investigate anything. If there are problems in this department, Congress should launch a thorough investigation and bring about reforms. In the meantime, test cases can be brought into federal court. The American Lutheran Church, through its leadership, structure, publications and membership of many talents, can encourage action to assist those seeking political asylum and could launch its own study to reexamine, redefine and strengthen the system.

There is the question of nonpayment of all or part of taxes

because the money is used for military or other objectionable purpose. Can anyone seriously believe that our nation can function if individual taxpayers direct where their tax payments shall or shall not go? Furthermore, it is an absolutely futile form of protest. A conscientious objector who refuses to go to war accomplishes something: he does not go. Those who refuse to pay taxes hurt only themselves, do not change the flow of one cent of public funds, and will wind up contributing more to the government they oppose. It would be far better to work for the passage of the World Peace Tax Fund Act, which would permit a taxpayer to have a proportion of his tax payment go into a trust fund for non-military peace-related activities.

Another issue is the matter of conscientious objection to military service on a selective basis, letting people decide in which war they will participate. I can understand a person's conscientious objection to war, and our laws permit alternative service. To choose which war to support and which not to support is, to me, not a moral but a political decision. I do not know how our country can function if people are going to have individual decision on which taxes to pay, which wars to support, which laws to obey.

It is not easy to provide social justice and preserve individual freedom. We have done well in the United States; we certainly need to strive to do better, and it is proper for the church to quicken the sensibilities of Christians to respond to human suffering and deprivation of every kind. But we should do nothing that tends to erode, or even appears to condone, destructive methods that undermine our basic tenet: that ours is a government of laws in which power is derived from the consent of the governed. If the governed are not satisfied, there are ample ways to make correction. It can be frustrating, but we never reach the point of last resort. Every effort is progress toward consensus.

—October 18 (or thereabouts), 1984

THE ARM OF LIBERTY

Strengthening the Arm of Liberty" was the theme chosen by the Boy Scouts of America for its fortieth anniversary celebration in 1949. It was also the title I gave to my address that fall, to the annual meeting of the Minnesota Valley Area of the Boy Scouts of America, at the Gustavus Adolphus College field house.

Scouting was important to me in those years. My elder son Tony, who was fourteen in 1949, was a member of Troop 17 at St. Anthony Park Congregational Church. I was the troop's scoutmaster. Scouting gave Tony and me some wonderful experiences. The high spot was the Boy Scout's National Jamboree at Valley Forge, Pennsylvania in 1952. Fifty thousand scouts and their leaders were there. General Dwight D. Eisenhower, soon to be a candidate for president, was our featured speaker. We camped and cooked in units of eight, the standard scout patrol number. You can imagine the size of the campground required for 50,000 scouts organized in units of eight. I was on the sanitation committee, and had the difficult job of encouraging the scouts to throw away each day's uneaten food. There was no refrigeration, and it was important to avoid dysentery and other food-borne illnesses.

The scouting movement was very strong at that time. It seems to be less so today. The Boy Scouts did themselves a disservice when they barred gay people from positions of leadership. They carried a defense of that policy to the U.S. Supreme Court, and in 2000, the Supreme Court upheld their position. That has resulted in some loss of support for the Boy Scout movement, and involved them in a controversy that's difficult to resolve. I believe the organization erred when it made a universal judgment relative to gay people, assuming they were different from others on matters of law enforcement and morality. Gay people are to be accepted, just as other people are. If they want to have a domestic partnership, they should be allowed to have it with the full benefits and responsibilities that are extended to people who are married.

What I tried to tell the scouts in 1949 is that we must be brothers to all humankind, and that we ought not discriminate against anyone. We are called to peaceful ways of coexistence.

One cannot think of that message today without being mindful of the cataclysmic events of September 11, 2001. The horrific attack on the World Trade Center and the Pentagon has had a profound influence on the country, in several ways. First came a desire for revenge. The second was enormous patriotic fervor, arousing feelings of love of country and a strong willingness to act to protect and preserve it. The third, and most durable, I am sad to say, is a feeling of living in fear. All public events have to be carefully scrutinized and guarded because of the fear of more attacks. Fear was a factor in the 2002 election, in which President George Bush's Republican allies won big victories.

I'm hoping that as we progress farther, we will find peaceful ways of rooting out the cause of these dreadful incidents, and lead people to understand and accept each other better. Americans don't know enough about Islam, and it's obvious that many adherents of Islam do not know enough about the American people and their principles. It is regrettable that our trend since the 9/11 attacks has been isolation-bent. That is contrary to where technology is leading us, which is toward unity of the world. The world grows smaller in communication time, travel time and in every other way.

America seems to be in a period of transition. I hope future historians will be able to record that the nation moved from the idealism of the Statue of Liberty, through the present isolation, and to a future in which Americans draw closer to the rest of the world, and foster greater understanding among all the world's peoples.

Here is some of what I told the scouts in 1949:

⏭ Some time ago when I was in New York City, I took a boat ride around Manhattan Island. We cruised near the Statue of Liberty, and I felt the tingling excitement and yet hushed reverence that accompanies many a visit to it.

Ever since it was completed, the Statue of Liberty has been a mecca for tourists and sightseers. Of greater significance has been the symbolism that has come to surround this mighty figure. A writer in a recent issue of *National* magazine expressed it well when he said, "Facing out to a pain-wracked world, she represents more than an imposing statue of copper and iron...(She) stands for the history of a people—for the co-mingling of men and women from everywhere, of nationalities and religions, of diverse political creeds and variously colored races, all living together in peace and harmony." It is an ideal not fully realized, but it is the conscious goal of every American.

The evening after I saw the great statue, a news item caught my eye. Visitors to the Statue of Liberty would be barred for one week while necessary repairs were made. The right arm of the statue was dangerously weak and must be strengthened before visitors could again be admitted. Time, storms, cold and sun had all taken their toll, even the chipping of metal by thoughtless tourists. The arm of liberty was weak; it had to be strengthened.

It set me wondering: just as the physical arm of the statue was weak, was not the figurative arm of liberty in this country also weak? Is there not evidence of needed repairs? How appropriate that the Boy Scouts of America should select as the theme for the fortieth anniversary crusade, "Strengthening the Arm of Liberty."

It takes no searching analysis to find elements of weakness in the present situation of our nation. The signs are on every hand. The strength of the family as the key unit in our society is obviously impaired. Divorce is on the increase; social service agencies are crowded with the children of broken homes and children of unmarried mothers. Pastors, priests and rabbis are unhappy at the spiritual indifference of the people, even though church membership grows. The education of our children has become a national problem, so inadequate have become the facilities and financial support to this fundamental activity. In industrial fields, mighty organizations are deadlocked in strikes, which, even as we speak, threaten economic paralysis. In national defense we have witnessed the spectacle of the top leaders in the armed forces that have been directed to work in unity and harmony, not even speaking to one another. It reflects a weakness in our military establishment that is alarming. To prolong the recital would be depressing. But let us not be unaware of the facts, and facing the facts, seek a solution.

Let us first revert to the principles on which our society of liberty was established. Few nobler sentiments have ever been expressed than the line in the Declaration of Independence, "We hold these truths to be self evident: that all men are created equal; that they are endowed by their Creator with certain unalienable rights; that among these are life, liberty and the pursuit of happiness." We do not argue the point, we do not offer logical reasons. "We hold these truths to be self evident." Peoples of the world for centuries had heard of the divine right of Kings, but there we proclaimed the nobility, the divinity, the essential importance of the individual man.

Our whole concept of self-government rests on the individual, and only as individuals measure up to this opportunity and responsibility can our way of life be maintained. If we are to strengthen liberty, we must strengthen the individual—there is no mass solution, no wholesale answer. How crucially important, then, is the work of the Boy Scouts of America—to work with individual boys to help build worthy citizens.

When a boy becomes a scout, one of the first things he learns is the scout oath: "On my honor, I will do my best to do my duty to God and my country, and to obey the scout law; to help other people at all times; to keep myself physically strong, mentally awake and morally straight."

A father once brought home to his young son a new jigsaw puzzle of the world. He wondered if his young son could put the puzzle together for he, as yet, knew little of geography, and the puzzle was not easy. Imagine his surprise then when his boy came to him very soon after starting work on the puzzle to say, "Dad, I've finished the puzzle, come and see it." The father asked his son how he could do it so quickly. The boy answered, "Well, Dad, I found that the world was on one side of the puzzle, but a picture of a man was on the other. I found that if the man was right, the world was right."

As we struggle on state, national, and world levels with problems of human relationships, seeking legislative panaceas, could we not learn from the young boy? "If the man is right, the world is right."

How does scouting work with the individuals to prepare him for life as a citizen in our republic? Does scouting tie in with the need? Dwight Ramsey, National Coordinator of Field Service of the Boy Scouts, has made an interesting summary. He begins by noting that all the activities of scouting aim at training the individual in self-reliance and resourcefulness.

But scouting's aims do not end there. Through its troop structure, scouting points out the significance of small groups of citizens, working together for the common good. It works in cooperation with other institutions—home, church and school—to present boys with consistent messages and opportunities. It teaches its members to say, "What can I give to my community, my country?" – not, what can I get. It builds mutual respect for one's fellow citizen, of whatever race, creed or national origin.

When he was an old man, someone asked the great scientist, Sir Humphry Davy, what he considered his most important discovery. "My most important discovery," he said, "was Michael Faraday." How true, for it was the little bootblack whom Davy encouraged in scientific study who became one of the great scientists of all time.

Do we fully appreciate the challenge of our work with boys? Imagine, if you will, the result for our nation's future, if the Boy Scout movement reached every lad in this land of ours, and inculcated in him the principles of scouting. Then, tomorrow, as industrialists, as labor leaders, as public officials, we would have men living the scout oath and law. Men, who on their honor wanted to do their best to do their duty to keep themselves physically strong, mentally awake, and morally straight. That prospect is the great challenge of scouting. That is our continuing opportunity.

—October 24, 1949

MATURITY OF MIND

I sometimes think that lives are like cathedrals. Both require many years and great effort to become fully formed and functional. To be born is to be given the miracle of opportunity. What one does with that opportunity initially depends on the care and skill of others. But rather quickly, we must seize our own opportunities. We build our own cathedrals, of greater or lesser durability, beauty and utility.

What makes the difference? I believe giving is at the essence. Giving one's self in service to others is the wellspring of life's satisfaction. The reward that comes from the getting of perishable material wealth is superficial and fleeting. It's like a ride on a roller coaster, up and down and soon over. Abiding happiness derives from knowing that one has had a share in making a better future for someone else.

Learning is essential, for without it, one's opportunity for effective service to others is curtailed. I'm always saddened when I hear about young people of ability who forego advanced education. I regret the attitude of older people who believe their learning days are over. It is in learning, at any age, that we refresh ourselves with new understanding, ability, and confidence for service.

The world that we come into is not a perfect place, but it is a place that affords every human being enormous opportunity for advancement and improvement. Every person can contribute to the world's betterment, and can experience true happiness in so doing. Those ideas were at the heart of my commencement address to Marshall High School's graduating class in 1953. Here is some of that message:

⏭ Tonight, I welcome you into the community. That may seem a strange thing to do when many of you were born in this city, and have lived in your present neighborhood all of your life. But I welcome you to the community in the sense that having graduated from high school, your status changes very considerably. To a greater degree than ever before, you will be on your own. You will be making your own decisions and assuming new responsibilities. Among those responsibilities will be a civic responsibility, which I hope will lead you to be informed about public matters affecting your city, your state and your federal government.

You might well ask, What about this broader community? What is the state of the world? I would tell you frankly that you could not have graduated from high school at a better time. You enter a wonderful world of great opportunity. You might say that not everyone would speak so highly of our present situation. Are not wars and hunger still with us, are there not social problems of family breakdown and delinquency, does not our government sometimes seem to fall short in responding to the needs of the people? Is it really such a wonderful world?

Indeed, the picture is not all rosy. This is a world of human beings. It is not a perfect world. I don't suppose it ever will be. But let me state a few facts for you about your own situation at this particular time.

Through the great developments in medical science, you can look forward to a longer life than any graduating class before yours. Further, due to the fact of your being in the graduating class of Marshall High School in St. Paul, in the state of Minnesota, in the great United States, you have great advantages. At no time in our own country before this, and nowhere else in the world today, may you reap so much of the world's material comforts for a given period of time of work. The great industrial development of the last seventy-five years has resulted in efficiencies of production that bring great value to every hour of man's work.

This is a moment of great opportunity in every field of human endeavor. In this year of 1953, we are on a great new threshold of scientific opportunity. The releasing of atomic energy is an awe-inspiring thing, but scientific research in that field remains in its rudimentary stage. Now will come years of study to harness and exploit this great energy resource. It is a resource so tremendous that the energy in the atoms in a flask of water, if properly released and channeled, could provide all the energy for heat and power that the city of St. Paul could consume for many years.

Far greater opportunities exist in the field of human relationships. A huge social upheaval has been taking place throughout the world during the last fifty years. Out of it, certain facts are emerging. One is that people are pretty much the same the world over. Where they differ it is largely due to environmental factors. We now know that no people in the world is particularly war-hungry, nor people who are particularly peace-loving. There are not people who are particularly vicious and others who are particularly kind. All people are divine. All people have similar hopes and aspirations. What is more logical than that we should live in a united peaceful world? Simply stated, that is the challenge of this generation. The United Nations is one faltering step toward one world.

The stability and maturity that you bring to life individually can contribute much to improved human relationships. Those of you who will make the most of the life before you will do so because you develop a maturity of mind as you go along. May I mention just a few of the keystones that reflect maturity of mind?

One is the desire to give. To give is expansive, a broadening of the soul. To get, to grasp, to want, are restrictive, exclusive thoughts and gestures. If you ask me what you are going to get from the world, I must respond that you are on the wrong track. If you tell me that you would like to devote your life to nursing, I would say God bless you, come along, there is great need for you. There will be great reward in life's richest satisfactions, because you have the fundamental first keystone—a mature mind. You seek to give, not to get.

Another quality of maturity is constantly seeking for information, constantly searching for truth, constantly acquiring skills. Some of you may be debating even tonight, Shall I go to work or shall I continue my education? There is only one answer to that question. Whatever your abilities, whatever your capacity, whatever your interest, get all the training and education that you can possibly get. It will bring you the richest return of usefulness and satisfaction. It may be in a professional pursuit, it maybe in a vocational pursuit. Whatever it is, get training, get more education. If you need financial assistance to continue your education or training, consult with your school authorities, look for opportunities. The talent that you may take lightly may be greatly needed in this world, and you not only deny yourself but you deny your community and society if you fail to develop it to the fullest degree.

In your life's journey, you will need counsel. You will need advice. You will find that things your parents have said will come back to you. You will recall many times clear pictures of high school teachers and the influence they brought to bear. One place where you can find the distilled wisdom and divine inspiration of generations is the Bible. You can learn no more profound lesson than the truth contained in simple statements from the Bible. "Seek ye first the kingdom of God and his righteousness, and all these things shall be added unto you." There is no more profound truth in man's experience. "Do unto others as ye would they would do unto you." The secret of world peace, the secret of family harmony, the secret of personal repose—all are in those few words. Wherever you go, a Bible is handy. When you need counsel or advice, try it, and believe it.

My devout wish for the Class of 1953 of John Marshall High School, for each of you individually, is that you will be worthy. Give to the world the best that you have and the best will come back to you.

—June 9, 1953

And so, in conclusion,

On several occasions in the 1960s, I ended addresses with a recitation of John Addington Symonds' uplifting, optimistic hymn, "The Human Outlook." It nobly describes all humanity's dreams of peace, prosperity and freedom. It remains my fervent hope for Minnesota and the world.

These things shall be: A loftier race
Than e'er the world has known shall rise
With flame of freedom in their souls,
And light of science in their eyes.

They shall be gentle, brave and strong,
They spill no drop of blood, but dare
All that may plant man's lordship firm
On earth and fire and sea and air.

Nation with nation, land with land,
Unarmed shall live as brothers free.
In every heart and brain shall throb
The pulse of one fraternity.

These things—they are not dreams—shall be
For happier men when we are gone;
These golden days for them shall dawn
Transcending all we look upon.

— John Addington Symonds